MOVING TO MAINE

MOVING TO MAINE

The Essential Guide
to Get You There and What
You Need to Know to Stay

Third Edition

VICTORIA DOUDERA

Camden, Maine

Published by Down East Books
A wholly owned subsidary of The Rowman & Littlefield Publishing Group, Inc.
4501 Forbes Boulevard, Suite 200, Lanham, Maryland 20706
www.rowman.com

Unit A, Whitacre Mews, 26-34 Stannary Street, London SE11 4AB

Distributed by NATIONAL BOOK NETWORK

British Library Cataloguing in Publication Information Available

Library of Congress Cataloging-in-Publication Data

Doudera, Vicki, 1961–
  Moving to Maine : the essential guide to get you there and what you need to
know to stay / Victoria Doudera. —Third edition.
      pages cm
  ISBN 978-1-60893-282-5 (paperback : alkaline paper) — ISBN 978-1-60893-
283-2 (electronic) 1. Maine—Guidebooks. 2. Moving, Household—Maine—
Handbooks, manuals, etc. I. Title.
  F17.3.D68 2015
  917.41'04—dc23

                                                                2015015743

∞™ The paper used in this publication meets the minimum requirements of
American National Standard for Information Sciences—Permanence of Paper
for Printed Library Materials, ANSI/NISO Z39.48-1992.

Printed in the United States of America

To Ed, my partner, on our continuing Maine adventure

CONTENTS

ACKNOWLEDGMENTS

I send out a heartfelt thank you to all those who shared their Maine experiences with me during the writing of this third edition. Thanks also to my readers from the past fifteen years who've told me in detail how *Moving to Maine* has helped to guide their Maine adventures.

I appreciate the assistance of all the great folks around the state who have aided my research, or graciously allowed me to include their photographs. The folks at Down East Books and Rowman & Littlefield are terrific to work with, and I thank them for their expertise. Special thanks to editors Michael Steere and Joe Miller. I wish to acknowledge the support of Camden Real Estate Company, and in particular, Scott Horty, for his help and advice with this new edition. And finally, thanks to my family, especially Ed. Maine wouldn't be my favorite place without you.

INTRODUCTION

You're Moving *Where?*

No matter where in the country I go, people I meet are curious about what it's like to live in Maine. From Florida to Fresno, folks are eager to hear about Maine's coastline, mountains, forests, clean cities, and neat small towns. To people "from away," this state sounds like paradise—until they remember our four-season climate. I remember one woman from New York—a state that packs its own wintery punch—asking me if it snowed here year-round!

This same curiosity led me to write the very first edition of this book back in 2000, and I'm here to say the state's allure has not abated. It seems to be that, outside of northern New England, people hear you're from Maine and you're liable to get some pretty interesting responses. There are those who get almost teary, who feel a nostalgia for a place they haven't visited, as well as people such as my New York friend, who shiver at the thought of a few flakes. Although national weather information is just a click of a mouse away, the notion that Maine is locked in the icy grip of winter for most of the year persists. You'd think this was the United States' version of the Arctic from the responses Maine can elicit. And then there is the geographical confusion. Just where in the world are we, anyway?

A group of Italians I encountered years ago in Florence had no reference point for Maine, and kept insisting the state was part of Vermont, despite my efforts to convince them otherwise. Finally, one of them had an epiphany. "Jessica Fletcher?" he queried, referring to Angela Lansbury's character on a popular television show from the 1980s called *Murder She Wrote.* Wearily I nodded and headed off to buy a gelato, leaving the group to reminisce about Hollywood's Cabot Cove and its many mysteries.

Maine isn't on the rest of the world's radar screen, except perhaps in TV reruns. Watch a game show and you'll see our fellow Americans scratching their heads trying to place it—I've had some people insist we were really part of Canada. Tucked way up in the northeastern corner of the country, Maine isn't a place you drive through, fly over, or happen upon unintentionally. So why in your wildest dreams would you ever want to live there?

In the nearly thirty years since I moved to Maine, I've learned that people come for as many reasons as there are lobster pots in Penobscot Bay or potatoes in an Aroostook field. An unsurpassed natural environment, a lifestyle that encourages a slower pace, a low rate of crime, and an economy that values creativity and entrepreneurship are just some of the lures. The affordability of real estate, especially when compared to other coastal states, is another.

There are people who move "back" to Maine, too. I think of them like wild salmon, swimming against the current to return to their roots and family. There are those who spent their college years here, or a military tour, and just never got the state out of their system. And then there are those who can't explain their reasons—they just know Maine is the place for them.

If you have recently relocated to Maine, are thinking about it, or have packed and labeled your boxes, this completely revised edition of *Moving to Maine* is for you. You'll find the answer to the big question (Why am I doing this?) as well as many others, such as:

- Is Maine part of mainstream America?
- Are there good-paying jobs up there that offer rewarding work?
- Can I live in a remote, rural state?
- Is there anyone under sixty?
- Will my business still prosper?
- Is there enough cultural and ethnic diversity? Is there any?
- Are there decent doctors? Schools? Restaurants?
- Can I survive the winter?
- Will my family find things to do?
- Will I ever really fit in?

Here is the scoop on what it's really like to live here. The biggest advantages. The surprising benefits. And even the pitfalls. With loads of useful information, helpful hints, and tips from those who've already blazed the trail, you'll learn how to manage in Maine before you step foot in the Pine Tree State.

If you've already made up your mind and taken on the 207 area code, you'll find the following chapters to be a useful guide to your new state. The information you need to get acquainted is here, including tips on everything from registering your car to eating a lobster, to rafting your first North Woods river.

MY STORY

Did I mention that some people move to Maine almost on a whim?

Maybe it's the benefit of hindsight, but when I look back at our reasons for moving north almost three decades ago, they seem pretty thin to me. Yes, I love the outdoors and knew I'd appreciate Maine's clean, natural environment. And yes, we thought small-town living in a close-knit community would be ideal as we started our life together. Did we know anyone in Maine? No. Had we taken several scouting trips, done our homework ahead of time? No. We'd been to Maine together only once, on a spontaneous drive up the coast to the fishing village of Corea, to rent a cottage I saw advertised in the *Boston Globe*—Talk about a whim! Take a look at your Maine map and you'll see how far we drove.

We didn't have jobs, or even a modest nest egg, or any real ties to the state. But we had something that many new Mainers possess: a spirit of adventure. Along with that, we shared a willingness to work hard and keep our minds open. We knew we were choosing the road less traveled, a path that not everyone would understand right away, but we felt in our hearts that it was our destiny. Thanks to the feedback I received from readers of past editions of *Moving to Maine*, I know that many of you take similar leaps of faith in coming here.

Our sense of adventure prompted us to drive from Boston to Maine on one of the coldest weekends of the winter in January of 1986. The mercury hovered in the single digits (Fahrenheit) as we purred along in Ed's aging Datsun 280Z, weaving our way up the coast, bundled in down and polar fleece as if on an expedition. We'd decided to look for a business and had even taken a class at Boston's Center for Adult Education on inn ownership. The teacher of the workshop was himself an innkeeper who did his best to prepare participants for the pitfalls of the hospitality industry. "You'll get divorced and become alcoholics," he warned. "That's what happened to me."

Despite his precautions, we made appointments and toured several turnkey properties in different parts of the state. Our intention was to buy a business, but it was a forlorn Victorian, empty and unkempt, that captured our interest. Beneath the house's grime and through the myriad cobwebs, we spied ornate plaster moldings and peeling tin ceilings, lovely old floorboards, and deep parlor fireplaces. Underneath it all we could see a lovely inn that we would breathe to life ourselves. As we stood shivering in the damp chill, that mysterious alchemy between old homes and romantic souls worked its magic, and we succumbed to the Victorian's hidden charms. Three months later, the house belonged to us and our Maine adventure had begun.

We barely had time to think about our new lives that first year. Renovating the house took months of sawdust and sweat, and then we were thrust headlong into the role of innkeepers. Ed baked muffins and flipped flapjacks, and in his spare time he passed the Maine Bar Exam. He opened a law practice in a pretty tin-ceilinged room at the front of the inn. We joined town committees and the church down the street, adopted a black lab puppy, and began to feel at home.

Yet it wasn't long before we noticed there were palpable differences to living in Maine, differences that went beyond the physical surroundings.

One day I was running some errands in the village. As I slowed at a blinking yellow light at one of the few intersections, a car horn began honking insistently at me. In a flash, my Boston-driver instincts kicked in. "Give me a break," I muttered. I scanned the streets for the offending car, ready to give its obviously obnoxious driver a nasty look, at the very least. There, idling on a side street, I found the culprit: an enthusiastic woman I'd met the day before, smiling and waving while sounding her horn.

Another day, I was in the supermarket checkout line with my cart full of inn supplies, when I realized my meager amount of cash wasn't nearly enough. I'd forgotten my checkbook and credit cards and I was ready to put the groceries back when an employee handed me a fifty dollar bill. I thanked him and asked if he wanted my name and address. "Nah," he said. "You'll pay me back."

These are the kinds of stories newcomers tell all the time, the kinds of tales that demonstrate the unexpected richness of life in Maine. When Ed and I fell under the spell of that old house years ago, we really became part of a place with much more to offer than we could have ever imagined. A place with people—some of them "natives" and some (like us) "from away"—who've become good friends. A state where our children—even now, when they are in their twenties and living elsewhere—are valued members of the community. A place where I can enjoy the outdoors to my heart's content. Personally, I couldn't agree more with the tourist slogan—Maine is "the way life should be."

Nevertheless, the nation's most northeasterly state is not for everyone. Living in the more remote sections or weathering the sometimes long winters can be a challenge. Making a living here takes some real resourcefulness. Taxes can seem comparatively high and ethnic diversity disappointingly low. Maine isn't perfect—what place is?—although some of us consider it a lot closer to perfection than anywhere else.

THIS BOOK

To get perspectives other than my own, I once again spoke with new residents who've moved here from all over the United States within the past few years. These kind souls shared their biggest challenges and rewards as new Mainers. "What do you wish you had known before you moved here?" I asked. Their thoughtful answers to my many questions helped me enormously in creating what I hope is a truly useful, informative guide.

In writing this updated edition, I've also had guidance from my readers. I truly appreciate the kind comments and constructive feedback you've shared, and I've done my best to incorporate your thoughts. One of the best conversations I had about the book was with a new Mainer who said he felt I had written *Moving to Maine* from my heart. I think he's correct. My heartfelt advice and that of others is within these pages.

One of the best things about writing a book like this is connecting with readers, and I hope I'll hear from you. When you have a chance, please visit my Web site at vickidoudera.com to send me an e-mail, see some of my other writing, or ask a Maine real estate question. I welcome and thank you for your comments and time.

I'll close with what I said back in 2000, when the first edition of *Moving to Maine* debuted: moving anywhere is an undertaking that requires courage, energy, creativity, and faith. For your move here, you might want to bring along bug spray and a warm jacket as well. And a snow shovel!

Best of luck to you as you begin your adventure in Maine.

1

THE SPIRIT OF MAINE

"I'm from Maine. I eat apple pie for breakfast."

—Rachel Nichols, actress, raised in Augusta

What is it about this state that pulls people here like metal to a magnet? Other than the traditional Maine breakfast of a generous slice of pie?

For many, it's the state's beauty—the rough-hewn coastline and rugged islands, the spruce-filled forests and towering mountains, the clean rivers, lakes, and streams. Carolyn Mahler, who moved to South Thomaston from Texas in 2013, fell in love with a description of Maine in a mystery novel and became hooked. Others, like Dorothy Paradis of Cornish, cite the relaxed pace of life in Maine. "I automatically shift into low gear the minute I cross the border into Maine," she says. "I love wearing shorts and sandals to work, seeing lots and lots of green, and making my own rules, hours, and goals."

For some, it's Maine's inhabitants who make the difference. "We love it here," says Paula Palakawong, who moved to the midcoast from Florida in 2010. "We really feel like we are part of a community."

"We also chose Maine for the people," says Lynda Chilton, who relocated from Virginia with her husband and children. "In the little bits of time we spent here, we made good friends. People I would have kept in touch with, even if we hadn't decided to move up. When you live in a metropolitan area, you get used to not having time for close friends, and the people you come in contact with in stores, restaurants, and in business are stressed out, and often surly and rude. Road rage invades all parts of life. In Maine, people take the time to be nice—you feel you are part of the community."

While I was drawn here by all of these things, I never dreamed I would discover an overriding state spirit, what former Senator Angus King calls "that indefinable attitude that won't take no for an answer, that says yes to life and its infinite possibilities." Although I had canoed down the Saco River and fished in Rangeley Lake, I thought of the state in a fairly stereotypical way: a vast expanse on top of New Hampshire, full of moose, lobsters, and tight-lipped New Englanders. Maine seemed too big and too wild to have its own distinct identity.

I settled in Maine and soon discovered—as do all newcomers who don't know it already—that Maine is a place with a soul, something that is felt more than seen. An attitude, a mystique, summed up in the sigh that escapes the lips when crossing the Piscataqua River at Kittery, regardless of how many times you've done it before.

THE ESSENCE OF MAINE

There is a palpable Maine spirit, no matter where in the state you go, a mixture of pride and perseverance sprinkled with independence and old-fashioned neighborliness. Mainers have "moxie," a term from the late 1800s meaning nerve and verve (and also the name of a century-old beverage, still popular around the region). Like the state's heroes—Civil War General Joshua Chamberlain, pioneering Senator Margaret Chase Smith, and former Governor Edmund Muskie, to name just a few—Mainers may be humble, but they aren't afraid to stand up for what's right.

Businesspeople who relocate to Maine from other states are often amazed by the strong work ethic here. The sun rises early in the Pine Tree State, and most Mainers have already had a mug or two of coffee before the rest of the country is out of bed. They also are exacting, and believe in quality and workmanship. Whether their field is biotechnology or blueberries, residents here comprise the best workforce in the country.

The Maine spirit creates an indelible impression on those who adopt the state as their home. Most newcomers find the indefinable attitude contagious and take it on themselves. Others see it as a precious commodity that might spoil if not tended: "Be prepared to be a part of Maine," advises newcomer Carol Doherty-Cox, who moved to Port Clyde from Westchester County, New York. "Don't bring your old life with you. The value of Maine is in its identity. We don't need to inundate the state with people who want to remake it in their image."

The Maine mind-set and lifestyle can come as a bit of a shock to new-comers. The rhythm of life is slower, and the frenetic pace of large cities (and even most suburbs) is not commonly found. "People aren't living off their calendars here," says Thad Chilton, a Virginia native. "Nobody pulls out their date book to make an appointment." Catching up on the latest news at the post office is viewed as more important than merely processing people through a line. Cashiers at stores—even large department chains—take time to chat or offer helpful advice about purchases. Newcomers who are used to a faster pace will find that patience is a virtue that can often come in handy here.

Maine is old-fashioned in other ways as well. Deals may still be sealed with a handshake, and issues are often worked out over the backyard fence rather than in the county courtroom. This is not a cynical, world-weary place—honesty and integrity are assumed to be part of everyone's makeup. "I love that you still see the honor system here at farm stands," says Paula Palakawong, referring to the little baskets at roadside vegetable stands where buyers place payment for choice zucchini and peppers.

"No one seems to be uptight about anything," agrees Jane Dahmen, a resident of Newcastle since 2005. "People have a good handle on what's important in life—but they are bright, interesting, talented, and they love living here. They are great neighbors."

The ways of the village flavor life even in the urban areas. When in need, Mainers depend on one another. Neighbors drop off fragrant chicken pot pies or hearty casseroles when a new baby comes; community suppers are held to raise money for families struggling with an illness or unexpected accident. This willingness to lend a hand was demonstrated to the rest of the nation during the state's great ice storm of 1998. Crews from as far away as North Carolina, here to fix downed lines, were astounded at the warm welcome they received from victims of the storm, many of whom had been without power for several days. Former Congressman Thomas H. Allen sums it up this way, "While Maine is populated by people who pride themselves on their self-reliance, we are also quick to help a neighbor or even a stranger in need."

In many ways, the state functions as one big small town. But despite this closeness, newcomers are warmly welcomed.

"We were concerned about being seen as outsiders, especially since that was how we were treated in South Carolina," says Mary Griffin of Orono. "But the Bangor region really welcomed and embraced us and made us feel as though we were part of a great community."

Kathleen and Robert Hirsch, former Pennsylvanians, concur. "We had always heard that if you weren't born in Maine you would always be 'from away.' Not only were we not natives, but we didn't even have a history of spending a lot of time in Maine. My big concern was whether we would ever be accepted. I even considered creating a tale about great-grandparents and grandparents living and vacationing in Maine to give us more credibility but I never got that story concocted. So, here we were living in Maine and the question everyone seemed to ask was, 'whatever brought you here to Maine?' There is no good answer to that question other than to say that Maine 'felt' like the right place for us to be. And now that we are here, we can actually say that it is a great place to be. My fears of not being accepted were ill-founded. We have found the people here to be warm, welcoming, and helpful."

Nan Rowe, who moved to rural Waldo County from Florida in 2013, agrees. "The myth that if you're not a third-generation Mainer you'll always be 'from away' is not relevant," she says. "All of my neighbors have been so welcoming to me. They don't care if I'm a native or not. I've never been treated like a different species."

PROFILE—PART OF A CREATIVE COMMUNITY

Ravin Nakjaroen and Paula Palakawong were the husband and wife owners of an upscale Thai restaurant in Fort Lauderdale when the economic downturn forced them to close. They came north to Maine for a job at an inn, and when that door closed in 2010, they opened another Thai restaurant—this time in Maine. Paula says the biggest surprise for them has been the old-fashioned community spirit she feels here. "It's like going back in time in some ways. People bring fruits or veggies to their neighbors; they actually make things by hand to thank people. It's not a trend here—this is the way people live." She says that in addition to this nostalgic feeling, she also appreciates the creativity of her community and the support it has given their restaurant, Long Grain. "We are all entwined here, in a good way. I ordered furniture from a shop in town, and they come here to eat. Our ingredients are locally sourced from area farms and we see those people as customers. We value that."

SOMETHING FOR EVERYONE

Maine's natural assets have always been its greatest attraction to vacationers, and they are a big lure for new residents as well. "One of the biggest advantages to living in Maine is the beautiful natural environment," says Lynda Chilton, a native of Virginia. "When I go anywhere here, my views are of beautiful mountains, oceans lapping at rocky shorelines, charming old homes, and comfortable farms."

Maine offers something for everyone, largely because of its size. Measuring 320 miles long by 210 miles wide, the state encompasses 33,215 square miles—about as much land area as all of the other five New England states combined. Its famous rocky coastline curves in and out for 3,478 miles, from York to Washington counties. It comprises sixteen counties with twenty-two cities, 424 towns, fifty-one plantations, and 416 unorganized townships. One county, Aroostook, is so big that it alone is larger than Connecticut and Rhode Island combined. Distances between Maine towns can be vast for travelers used to the scale of southern New England. For instance, Portland, the state's largest city, is actually closer to New York City (328 miles) than to Madawaska on the Canadian border (356 miles).

Maine boasts 542,629 acres of state and national parks, including Acadia National Park, Baxter State Park, and the ninety-two-mile Allagash Wilderness Waterway. The state's highest peak, Mt. Katahdin, rises almost a mile above sea level, while Acadia's Cadillac Mountain has the distinction of being the tallest mountain on the eastern seaboard.

Water abounds in Maine—on a map the state appears to be sinking, so frequently do blue patches interrupt the green! There are thirty-two thousand miles of rivers and streams, fifty-one lakes that have an area of at least five miles, and, of course, the meandering coastline. More than three thousand islands dot the bays, making for spectacular sailing. Pleasure boats of all sizes ply the waters, as do working lobster and fishing vessels, ferries, and the beautiful historic wooden schooners called windjammers. "For me, spending time on the coast of Maine was truly magic," says Lynda Chilton. "I felt that this place was calling to me and my family."

THE PEOPLE OF MAINE

Ask new residents in Maine why they like living here, and, without fail, they will mention their neighbors. Mainers may be gruff or loquacious, natives or relative newcomers, yet almost all of them share a sense of community and a love for their state and its resources. "People here are friendly and supportive," says Dottie Paradis, who moved to Cornish from Massachusetts. "Not at all the staunch and rigid Yankees I imagined."

Even those who have been here for several decades cite Mainers themselves as a draw. "I met a man who said he moved here twenty-five years ago," says Kathleen Hirsch. "He said he chose Maine for the people and he has stayed here because of the people. That says you can't go wrong moving to Maine!"

Carole Brand, who came to Maine in 2005, has formed a theory concerning why residents are typecast as rough-and-tumble woodsmen. "The stereotype of Mainers as mostly backwoods loggers in red flannel shirts living in drafty log cabins who drive trucks, drink beer, think ice fishing is the height of culture, and whose vocabulary consists of the all-purpose 'Ayuh' is locally promulgated as a way of keeping the tourist population in check. In fact, my immediate neighbors consist of a nuclear physicist, a retired pediatric oncologist, a pathologist, a former executive of Rockefeller Institute, a computer scientist, and a retired mathematics professor. The annual conference on foreign policy was sold out within days, and I am having difficulty finding a book group that has an opening. However, the local Shakespeare Society has been very welcoming."

Approximately 1,328,302 people live in the state of Maine in an estimated 503,224 households. The majority of them call the countryside home. While nearly 80 percent of the population of the United States lives in metropolitan areas, less than 40 percent of Mainers live in cities. Maine has three urbanized areas—Portland, Bangor, and Lewiston—and twenty-four urban clusters, ranging in size from Calais (population 2,504) to Brunswick (population 29,159).

In 2010, Maine beat out Vermont as the most rural state, changing places over the last decade. According to the Census Bureau, 61.1 percent of Vermont's population lived in rural areas in 2010. In 2000, Vermont was the most rural state at 61.8 percent and Maine was second at 59.8 percent. Maine bucked the national trend by becoming more rural over the last decade.

People here like their personal space. The average population density is sixteen persons per square mile, and, in about half the state, this figure drops to only one person per three square miles. More than one-half the population of Maine lives in the southern or southwestern corner of the state.

WHO LIVES HERE?

To better answer the question of who lives in Maine today, let's take a look back at the very first folks who took the Maine plunge. The earliest permanent European settlers here came from western England. They were soon followed by the Scots-Irish and by a number of Quakers, or Friends, from the other New England colonies. In the 1740s Germans settled in Waldoboro, and soon afterward many Irish Roman Catholics moved to York, Lincoln, and Cumberland counties. The French, who controlled much of Maine's territory until 1759, were not active colonists early on, although a number of families of French Huguenots settled along the coast.

The 1800s brought large-scale emigration westward as cheap land and gold strikes lured Mainers away. So great was the human "outflow" in 1870 that William W. Thomas, the state commissioner of immigration, brought over a group of Swedish immigrants who established the colony of New Sweden in northern Aroostook County. Although Maine has a slightly higher number of English, Irish, Scotch, Dutch, and German ancestors than the United States as a whole, one group of immigrants would arrive in the late nineteenth century to work in industry and forever alter the state's cultural mix: the French.

"The most outstanding feature of ancestral composition in Maine is the large percentage of French," says a report from the Maine Department of Labor called "Diversity and Community." "From a national point of view, this large French concentration is unique. Over time the French have shown the least inclination of all other European countries to migrate and have typically had the highest rates of return."

Today, there remain large numbers of people of French American descent in much of Maine, particularly in the Lewiston-Auburn, Biddeford-Saco, and Augusta-Waterville areas. An American Community Survey compiled from 2008 to 2012 finds that 16.9 percent of Mainers claim French ancestry, while nationwide the percentage is 2.9. Maine's French immigrants were eventually joined in the industrial centers by Finns, Russians, Poles, Italians, and others from southern and eastern Europe. However, none of these settlers were the region's earliest modern inhabitants. The Wabanaki Indians, or "People of the Dawnland," first called Maine home. Their tribes include the Passamaquoddies, Penobscots, Maliseets, and Micmacs. Native Americans in present-day Maine belong to either the Passamaquoddy or Penobscot tribe, and comprise approximately 0.6 percent of the total population. The Penobscot reservation is on Indian

Island, in the Penobscot River near Old Town, and the two Passamaquoddy reservations are in Washington County.

Mainers are very proud of their ethnic roots, and fairs, festivals, celebrations, and religious observances honor the origins of the state's many
cultures. Bagpipes play at the Highland Games in Brunswick, and the lilting
sounds of traditional French chansons fill the air in Lewiston and Auburn
at the Festival de Joie. Midsommar Festival, held in the Aroostook County
towns of New Sweden and Stockholm, commemorates that area's Swedish
heritage, and a day honoring Maine's Wabanaki tribes occurs in April. Despite these celebrations, almost all newcomers, like Laura Read of Arundel,
feel Maine is still rather homogenous culturally, lacking a blend of cultures,
races, and religions. "There are very few people of color," she notes. Adds
Peter Mahncke of Kingfield, "I love Maine's beautiful landscape, the slower
pace, the tranquility, and the ability to use the land for recreational pur-
poses. The only downside to living in Maine might be that the population
isn't very diverse."

GROWING DIVERSITY

It's true that the face of Maine is largely white—95.3 percent in 2012—but
that percentage is slowly—but consistently—changing. Although Maine
ranks just behind Vermont as the whitest state in the nation, census figures
indicate that the Pine Tree State is becoming more racially and culturally
diverse. Ethnic populations increased in all sixteen counties between 2000
and 2010, and the Census Bureau predicts that this growth will continue.

According to data compiled by Harvard School of Public Health, the
state's three largest urban areas—Bangor, Lewiston-Auburn, and Portland-
South Portland—saw gains during the past decade of 6.2 percent, 3.8
percent, and 5.4 percent, respectively, in the percentage of residents who
identify their ethnicity as something other than non-Hispanic white.

"Focusing on Maine's relatively small share of diversity can obscure
the changes that have been occurring," Charles Colgan of the Muskie
School of Public Service said in a 2012 article in the *Bangor Daily News*.
He noted that because the state is so predominantly white and older—with
slow population growth—cultural change occurs at a slower rate.

And yet racial diversity has always existed in Maine. Native Americans are the original inhabitants of the state, and African Americans were
living in Maine by the early 1600s. Racial diversity in Maine is growing
today because of births in families of color and for reasons seen throughout

history—people's migration in search of economic opportunity and a safe place to live and raise families. That migration includes foreign refugees who are settling here, as well as native-born people of color coming for jobs and Maine's quality of life.

Like other rural areas around the country, Maine's cultural integration has been greatly boosted on a virtual level by the Internet. Students using laptops in the state's middle and high schools can forge connections, and working Mainers can draw upon ideas and contacts from all over the world.

But while technology can close the gap, it is not the same as living in a culturally diverse environment. Maine—like the rest of American society—is on its way to becoming more multihued, multilingual, and multiethnic—but a slower pace.

Statistics show that much of Maine's recent ethnic and religious diversity has come through the United States Refugee Resettlement Program. Since 1975, Catholic Charities Maine, the major organization designated for refugee resettlement in the state, has assisted in the resettlement process for over five thousand refugees from some twenty-five countries in Southeast Asia, Africa, the Near East, Eastern Europe, Cuba, and the former Soviet Republics, including Cambodia, India, Vietnam, Afghanistan, Somalia, the Sudan, the Democratic Republic of Congo, Iran, Iraq, and Russia. This program has considerably grown the cultural and religious diversity in Maine. In particular, Buddhists and Muslims from these countries have planted their roots, creating religious centers and participating in the civic, social, and economic life of Maine.

"Religious diversity can increasingly be found in the smallest and most unexpected pockets of America's geographic and civic landscape," says Colleen Rost-Banik, a member of the Pluralism Project, part of Harvard University's Committee on the Study of Religion. "Maine is one such pocket." She notes that aside from refugees bringing their religious and cultural heritage with them, the landscape is also a draw for religious diversity. "Maine's beaches, mountains and rolling hills have helped give rise to a number of religious communities—from Baha'is who began the internationally known and visited Green Acre Baha'i School along the beautiful banks of the Piscataqua River; to the Buddhists, many of whom have moved to Maine from neighboring cities on the East Coast and started meditation groups in their homes so that they can practice in a more relaxed atmosphere; to the pagans who have been supported in both solitary and community practice by the vast spaces of land and water all throughout Maine."

The Pluralism Project's report notes that while religious diversity is on the rise all over the United States, what makes Maine unique is the level of interconnectedness among religious and civic institutions. "Since there is such a small population in the state, many people realize that in order to coexist and accomplish the goals needed to move Maine forward, all groups of people must be actively engaged in the public square. The state of Maine, which is quite large in landmass, is actually a small community with few degrees of separation among people. When resources are limited, and when a community understands that all its realms are interconnected, they realize they must work together for their collective well-being."

Maine's service organizations, school systems, and religious communities collaborate to make sure that the various needs of people are met. Notes Rost-Banik, "In one instance, when the Portland Muslim community struggled to find a space that was big enough and willing to host their Eid al-Adha prayer, a local public school opened up their gymnasium to the community. Some might contend that this blurs the line of separation between church and state. But in reality, the public school system is working to ensure that underrepresented communities have the same resources afforded to more privileged groups in the area."

What is it like to be a minority in Maine? The reactions are mixed: some newcomers who are non-white feel comfortable here, especially in the more multicultural urban centers, while others sense a lack of acceptance. Shay Stewart-Bouley, who writes the "Diverse-City" column for the *Portland Phoenix* and blogs at BlackgirlinMaine.com, says, "Maine is a four-season place, it's a fun place but it's also a pretty homogenous state though that is slowly changing. Most black people and people of color in general in Maine tend to live in the Southern part of the state with most of us concentrated in the Greater Portland area. Maine is not a state plagued with a racist past, but it is a state where meeting people who have little contact with people of color is not that uncommon. That said, Mainers are a pretty open and accepting bunch. My experience is once people know you and know what you are about, your race, sexual orientation, whatever is not an issue. But change is sometimes uncomfortable."

Sonya Arguijo Frederick says that the lack of diversity can personally be tough to take. Having moved here in 2013 from Chicago, she says that for the first time in her life, she feels like a minority. "I feel different and I even had someone tell me she was glad our family was here because we needed more 'browns' in Maine. I didn't know whether to laugh or cry."

Attitudes toward issues of sexual orientation have been easier to measure, with Mainers rejecting an effort to repeal the state's gay-rights law, allowing Maine to join the other New England states in legally protecting homosexuals from discrimination. In November of 2005, Mainers went to the polls to approve the sexual orientation and gender identity non-discrimination bill which had passed both houses of the Maine Legislature with strong bipartisan margins and was signed into law by then-Governor John Baldacci. The law exempts religious organizations that do not receive public funds, and is worded to say it is not meant to address a right to marry. Maine is the sixteenth state overall to outlaw discrimination based on sexual orientation and the sixth state to outlaw discrimination based on gender identity.

Same-sex marriage in Maine became legal on December 29, 2012. The bill for legalization was approved by voters, 53 percent to 47 percent, on November 6, 2012, as Maine, Maryland, and Washington became the first U.S. states to legalize same-sex marriage by popular vote. Election results were certified by the Maine Secretary of State's office and Governor Paul LePage on November 29. The 2012 referendum was a reversal of action on a similar bill three years earlier.

Ian Grady, a spokesperson for Equality Maine, has said there is still work to do in Maine. "Work to make sure kids feel safe in school the matter who they are, work to make sure that LGBT elders don't have to go back into the closet when they're going into assisted living centers, and work to make sure LGBT people in any town in Maine from Portland to Presque Isle feel safe and healthy living their lives authentically as the people they are."

Like any other state, Maine is also exposed to diversity of all kinds as influences continue to permeate popular culture, music, current events, film, and television. "Maine is a state that embraces tolerance," former Governor John Baldacci has said, "and it will thrive based on a celebration of each individual's diverse strengths."

On a recent trip to Nashville, Tennessee, a cab driver saw my Maine sweatshirt and began telling me how much his relatives loved living in Portland. "My cousins are refugees from Somalia," he told me. "They say the people there are very, very nice. It is a city that acts like a small village." Most Mainers—no matter what their ethnic origin—believe the state will benefit as diversity here grows.

SLOW POPULATION GROWTH

Maine's population on the whole is growing, albeit slowly. From 2000 to 2010, Maine's population grew by 4.2 percent. Who's moving in? All kinds of people, really—young families, early retirees, skilled professionals, risk-taking entrepreneurs. They come from all over the map, although migration from southern New England and the mid-Atlantic region outnumbers other spots.

The northeastern United States has historically been a source for Maine's new residents. Many Maine towns were settled in the 1700s by families from Massachusetts or New Hampshire seeking cheap land and abundant game. A century later, the so-called rusticators (moneyed summer residents of Bar Harbor, Kennebunkport, Islesboro, and other coastal communities) boarded steamships to escape the heat of their home cities of Philadelphia, Boston, and New York City. And many of their families liked it here so much that they settled in Maine permanently.

But certainly not everyone is from the Northeast. Ruth Anne and Wesley Hohfeld came to Maine in 2001 from California. "We wanted to move out of the high pressure San Francisco Bay area," says Ruth Anne. "We wanted a lower cost of living and less people." Laura Read lived in North Carolina and came to Maine to work at a summer camp. "I loved the blunt personality of Mainers," she says. "So refreshing compared to the 'Southern Gals' I grew up with." Jeff and Cathy Cleaveland moved to the small town of Appleton from Seattle. "We wanted to be on the East Coast, closer to family in Massachusetts," says Cathy. While she loves having lots of land and four distinct seasons, there's one thing Cathy misses about Seattle: "Drive-through coffee stands!"

AN AGING POPULATION

Maine's—and the world's—populations are aging. Maine's median age is 41.2, almost five full years above the United States' and about thirteen years higher than the country's youngest state, Utah. A sizeable number of Baby Boomers, combined with a decreasing younger population and relative lack of immigrants, mean this trend will likely continue. Experts say the state's older population is projected to increase from 14.4 percent to 26.5 percent of the population, while at the same time, the proportion of Mainers under eighteen will fall from 23.6 percent to 18.1 percent.

Maine is certainly not unique in this situation, but what are the implications of this trend for those of us who live here? Are there benefits to an older society? And what is it like to live here if you are under the median age?

"There's a lot of energy here now, from all ages," says Ben Fowlie, a thirty-something entrepreneur who lives in the midcoast. Josh Gerritsen, in his thirties and living in Lincolnville, agrees. "Even though there are less young people here than in New York City, you will meet wonderful people your age that make living here feel like paradise."

Retirees can bring good things to small towns, such as more walkable neighborhoods, a volunteer pool, and sizeable retirement incomes.

Not to mention the possibility of new jobs. Demographers see the graying of Maine's population as the potential beginning of a natural progression toward attracting young people and new families to the state. Since those groups are the most mobile demographics in the country, moving where jobs are readily available, Maine's aging population may in fact become a boon.

WHO IS A NATIVE?

With new people coming to Maine from just about everywhere, some good-natured speculation goes on concerning who is rightfully a "native." Strictly speaking, Maine natives have ancestral ties to the state going back at least three generations. It gets confusing because sometimes folks will answer the "Are you a native" question with, "Yep. Born and bred." But to many sticklers, merely being *born* in Maine isn't enough. Here's the succinct explanation you're likely to encounter: Just 'cause the cat has kittens in the oven, that don't make 'em biscuits.

It's all in fun, though—after all, folks "from away" have been coming to Maine for centuries. I like the old joke in which the fellow from Massachusetts asks the Mainer, "Have you lived here all your life?"

To which the Mainer answers, "Not yet."

No matter where you live in the state, your neighbors may be from just about anywhere: Veazie or Virginia, Scotland or Scarborough.

A SAFER PLACE TO BE

In addition to scenic beauty and welcoming people, Maine boasts something that, unfortunately, few other states can claim: friendly streets and neighborhoods. "We haven't locked our car doors in three years," says a former Californian. "We feel safe when we're out with our kids. My internal early warning radar system doesn't have to be on all the time. In fact, it's funny: every time I see a thriller or mystery at the movies, the setting is usually a gritty, urban environment. When I leave the theater, my city-tough attitude is on, and I look around corners for danger and generally have my bristles out. But then I quickly realize that's unnecessary and laugh at myself."

While law enforcement officials are quick to recommend street smarts even in the smallest town, the fact remains that crime in Maine is tame compared with other places. The state consistently ranks among the ten safest states, and in recent years, Maine has made the top three, coming in first in 2012. According to the Uniform Crime Reports, compiled by the FBI, the 2011 rate of violent crimes (murder, forcible rape, robbery, and aggravated assault) in Maine was 1.23 offenses per 1,000 people. The 2011 national average was 3.8 violent crimes per 1,000. Contrast that statistic with those of a few other states (Tennessee's rate of 6.08 or Florida's of 5.15), and you get a sense why newcomers feel appreciably more secure in Maine.

FOUR-SEASON CLIMATE

Although some might shiver at the very thought of the long winters, there are plenty of people who consider the Pine Tree State's climate to be ideal, and consider it part of the appeal of living here. "Frankly, I think the weather is an advantage," says Carole Brand. "Summers are cool and winters are very manageable."

"Maine is recognized as one of the most healthful states in the nation," claims the state tourism bureau. Smog-free air and moderate temperatures (average 70 degrees in summer, 20 degrees in winter) benefit residents whether working or playing. "I love the change of seasons," says Elizabeth Burrell, of Rockland. "The weather in California was so predictable."

And what of the legendary winters? While they offer an excellent chance to wear colorful fleece jackets and down parkas while pursuing a wide range of cold-weather sports, winters here tend to be the victims of hazy memory and hyperbole. For the most part, the force of old man winter in Maine has been greatly exaggerated. Data suggest that although the winters are frosty, prolonged severe cold spells are rare. "I find the winters invigorating," says Lynda Chilton. "Especially because I enjoy outdoor activities in all seasons."

We'll take a look at Maine's climate and delightful seasons (including winter) in more detail in chapter 6. You'll discover then that the weather— along with safer streets, caring people, and beautiful scenery—are all reasons to call Maine home.

MAINESPEAK

While only 7 percent of the population speaks something other than English at home, you may find your new neighbor's diction nevertheless different. Here's a little glossary of Down East expressions you won't find in your Webster's, as well as tips on how to master your own Maine accent:

Apiece	an undetermined distance
Ayuh	okay
Bug	lobster
Chowdered Up	destroyed
Crittah	furry animal
Cunnin'	cute
Dooryard	front yard
Finest Kind	the very best
From Away	not from Maine
Gawmy	clumsy
Numb	stupid
Pot	lobster trap
Prayer Handle	knee
Quahog	thick-shelled clam (pronounced co-hog)
Scrid	a tiny piece
Steamers	clams
Wicked	very

The secret to speaking like a Mainah? Relax your jaw. Let your lower jaw drop on the second syllable, pronouncing "er" at the end of a word as "ah." While you're at it, drag out some one-syllable words into two syllables. ("Here" becomes "hee-ah.") Drop the "g" in "ing" so that "running" becomes "runnin'." Finally, broaden "a" and "e" sounds, almost like the Brits, saying "cahn't" instead of "can't."

ONLY IN MAINE

Maine towns often appear on lists of the best places in the nation to live and do business. Here are a few examples:

- Deer Isle was chosen as the country's fifth-best small art town by John Villani in *The 100 Best Small Art Towns in America*. Belfast ranked tenth, and Lewiston came in at nineteenth.
- Brunswick was chosen as one of the top five places to retire by *Money Magazine* in June 2000.
- Portland made the list of "Ten Great Adventure Towns" in the September 2004 issue of *National Geographic Adventure Magazine*. That same year, *INC. Magazine* included Portland in its listing of the top twenty-five cities for doing business in America.
- Lincolnville was chosen as a top "American Dream Town," by *Outside* magazine in 2004.
- Bangor landed in the number two spot in the 2004 edition of "Cities Ranked & Rated." Bangor was found to be the second best location in the country among metropolitan areas with populations less than 100,000.
- Portland ranked as the number one large market in the country for small business vitality by *American City Business Journals* in January 2005.
- Rockland is ranked among the top one hundred best small towns to live in by *Outside Magazine*; and Lincolnville as one of the top one hundred best small towns to recreate in.
- Portland was rated one of the top ten cities to "Have It All" by the A&E television channel. Maine's largest city is consistently rated as one of the most desired cities to live in America.
- Camden was chosen one of the "50 Best Places to Live" by *Men's Journal* in 2006 for its growing cache as a telecommunity.
- Blue Hill was chosen by *Coastal Living* as a top beach town in June 2007.
- The U.S. Chamber of Commerce in its June 2011 report, *Enterprising States*, ranked Maine number one in infrastructure

and in the top ten in all three infrastructure measures—the share of high speed internet connections, the penetration of broadband by census tract, and a composite index of transportation infrastructure.

🌲 Brunswick was named by *Smithsonian Magazine* in its May 2012 edition as one of America's "20 Best Small Towns."

🌲 In 2013, Google named Scarborough the state's first e-City, for the strong Internet presence of its business community.

🌲 In 2014 Portland made *Time* magazine's list of cities "Getting it Right." The magazine named Portland to a list of nine cities with a thriving economy, a booming cultural scene, quality health care, and a growing university.

2

MAINE 101

"Maine is a joy in the summer. But the soul of Maine is more apparent in the winter."

—Paul Theroux, writer, graduate of the University of Maine

How does the Pine Tree State operate? A quick look at the natural features and history of the nation's most northeasterly corner goes a long way toward understanding how the state functions on a day-to-day basis.

MAINE GEOGRAPHY

Maine is diverse—geographically speaking—thanks to the work of massive glaciers long ago. As the slow-moving masses of ice crawled southeast, they scraped and softened the contours of mountains, gathered loose soil and stones, and broadened and deepened river valleys. When the climate warmed again, beginning fourteen thousand years ago, the glacier unloaded rocks, stone, and soil as it melted, creating moraines, eskers, and drumlins as well as the bodies of water dotting the state. Ancient river valleys were dammed up, forming chains of lakes, such as those in Belgrade. The weight of the mile-thick ice sheet had depressed the land, so when the glaciers melted and sea level rose, water flooded the sunken terrain, forming Maine's bays, inlets, and coves. Today's islands are the hilltops and ridges of this "drowned coast." Because of the glaciers, Maine contains the only fjord on the east coast—Somes Sound—and even, believe it or not, has its own stretches of "desert" in places like Freeport and Wayne, where erosion has exposed ancient deposits of glacial sand.

Maine's varied topography is something many new residents appreciate. "I think my favorite thing is the variety of terrain that we have," says Amy Bottomley, a resident of Bethel since 2011. "We have the mountains and skiing and hiking, but a couple of hours' drive east and we have beautiful harbor towns and the ocean."

A LITTLE HISTORY

Prehistoric inhabitants of Maine included Paleo Indians, who lived here perhaps 11,500 years ago. Historians believe they were followed by the Archaic Indians, and finally by the Red Paint People, whose artifacts, colored with distinctive red ochre, have been found on North Haven Island and elsewhere.

Evidence indicates that these natives enjoyed many of the same pleasures that present-day vacationers do. They headed to the coast in the summer for cool breezes and hearty seafood feasts. The middens, or piles of shells, they left behind are remnants of ancient clambakes. In addition to shellfish, they enjoyed porpoise and seal meat—items that have not remained a part of our modern summer menu.

When the first Europeans arrived is still a controversial topic. Debate rages over whether or not Vikings had a settlement in Maine. W. Hodding Carter, trip leader of the 1998 *Snorri* expedition, which traced the Vikings' route in a replica of a Norse ship, says, "We know for sure they were in Greenland and Newfoundland. We aren't certain they sailed to Maine. But after three months in a replica of a Viking merchant ship, I'm convinced that any self-respecting Viking would have found his way to Penobscot Bay."

An ancient Norse penny found in Brooklin, Maine, adds weight to Carter's sentiments. Dating back to 1065 or so, it's the oldest European artifact ever found in North America. The coin resides at the Maine State Museum in Augusta, although it is currently on display at the Smithsonian Institution.

EUROPEAN EXPLORATION

The first Europeans to "discover" Maine came in search of gold, spices, and the elusive Northwest Passage to the Orient, as well as more practical items such as fish, furs, and lumber. Beginning in 1524, Italian, Spanish, French, and English explorers traded along the coast, sailing home with full cargoes of valuable furs, cedar, and sassafras root, as well as stories of abundant fish and enormous lobsters.

Maine's first European settlers were a band of eighty Frenchmen, led by Sieur de Monts and Samuel de Champlain. They landed on St. Croix Island in the St. Croix River (notable for having the highest tides in the continental United States) in late June of 1604. The area was part of the region known as La Cadie, today called Acadia. After a dreadful winter, during which nearly half of the party perished, the Frenchmen pulled up stakes and headed to a more hospitable climate—Nova Scotia.

Throughout the seventeenth century, explorers came and went, including some of the more famous names from New England history, like Captains John Smith and Miles Standish. Smith landed on Monhegan Island in Muscongus Bay in 1614. He made Monhegan his home base for several years, and penned a bestseller about the region's attributes. Smith was the first to refer to Maine and the environs as New England rather than New Virginia, as it was first designated.

Soon the wild mainland bordered by islands came to be known simply as "Maine," and no one has been able to definitively say where the name came from. Some suggest it was derived from the term "mainland," others that it came from a French province. Although few Europeans lived here, the region was carved into huge tracts of land that were granted to wealthy English noblemen by the king. These land grants remained virtually unpopulated until the mid-1600s, when the successful Massachusetts Bay Colony began expanding, first into New Hampshire, and then northward into the "Province of Maine." In 1641, York, located on Maine's southern coast, became the first chartered city in America.

The hardy families who cleared the land, fished the sea and lakes, and began new lives in Maine were technically part of the colony—and later, state—of Massachusetts. From the beginning, though, their lifestyles and attitudes exhibited the independent spirit that is still strong in Maine. Native Americans, lumberjacks, mill owners, ice cutters, sea captains, fishermen—their colorful stories unfold in museums located throughout the state.

Maine remained part of the Commonwealth of Massachusetts until 1820, when papers were signed in Freeport to make it into a separate state. The twenty-third state, Maine came into the Union as part of the historic Missouri Compromise, a turning point in the nation's ongoing debate over slavery. (The "compromise" provided that Maine would be admitted as a free state, balanced by Missouri as a slave state.)

Statehood marked the beginning of another chapter in Maine's history, a story as rich and colorful as a prize-winning blueberry pie. To savor more than this small slice, try historian Neil Rolde's highly readable volume, *Maine: A Narrative History*.

A QUICK TOUR OF THE STATE

Maine is divided into sixteen counties. To best understand the state—and to get where you're going—a dependable map is key. The DeLorme Company's atlases, maps, and guides are known throughout the world for their reliability and quality, and many Mainers consider them indispensable, especially the *Maine Atlas and Gazetteer*. Besides showing Maine in painstaking detail, down to the last logging road, the *Atlas* is chock-full of information, from driving distances to state parks and canoe routes. It's available throughout the state at bookstores, supermarkets, and sporting-goods stores, or directly from the Yarmouth company at (800) 452-5931. Drop by their headquarters and see the massive globe Eartha or visit their Web site at www.delorme.com for more information.

POLITICS

State Government

Like many states, Maine has three governing branches: executive, legislative, and judiciary. The head of the executive branch is the governor, elected to a term of four years. The governor can serve no more than two consecutive terms, and the state does not have a lieutenant governor. If the governor dies or becomes unable to govern, the succession passes to the president of the senate and next to the speaker of the house.

The Maine legislature is composed of the House of Representatives and the Senate. The Maine House of Representatives consists of 151 members (one of the largest in the country) plus two nonvoting members representing the Penobscot Nation and the Passamaquoddy Tribe. Each house member represents a district of approximately 8,132 people.

The Maine Senate is the upper chamber and serves as the final confirming body of all bills passed before they are sent to the governor. There are thirty-five senators, and at this writing, nine are women. Compared to other states, Maine's had a high percentage of women elected to the senate, and has had the distinction of being the only state to have three women holding senate leadership positions during the same session. But we're used to such milestones. Back in 1964, Maine's Senator Margaret Chase Smith became the first woman in U.S. history to seek the presidential nomination of a major party.

Elected to two-year terms, the legislators pass the laws, confirm judges, and choose four constitutional officers, who also serve two-year terms: attorney general, secretary of state, state treasurer, state auditor. The effect of this procedure is to allow the majority party to control the constitutional offices.

Maine is one of three states with a joint standing budget committee system. The state budget must receive a two-thirds vote of the legislature, and the governor does not possess line-item veto power.

The judicial branch is headed by the Supreme Judicial Court, with a chief justice and six associate justices to handle appeals from lower courts. Criminal and court cases requiring a trial by jury are heard by the Superior Court, while civil actions, traffic infractions, juvenile cases, and small claims are heard in district courts, comprised of thirty-six judges who hold court in thirteen districts at many locations throughout Maine. Each county has a probate court to handle wills, estates, adoptions, and appointment of guardians. Probate in Maine, unlike in other states, is considered a simple, prompt, and relatively inexpensive process.

Local Government

Government in Maine, as in much of New England, has a strong local bias, with the town unit at its foundation. Towns (currently there are 432) must be incorporated, requiring a legislative act but not a charter. Towns are governed by the quintessential example of direct democracy—the annual town meeting and elected officials called selectmen. Since 1970, towns in Maine have operated under home rule, which means they may make many of their own decisions without going before the state legislature.

Maine's cities, numbering twenty-two, must be chartered by the legislature. All have a representative form of government called the city council. Population size doesn't always indicate city or town status. Eastport, in Washington County, for example, is a city of less than two thousand citizens, while Brunswick, with a population of more than fifteen thousand, is a town.

In addition to cities and towns, Maine still has examples of plantations, an archaic form of local government used centuries ago in Massachusetts.

Plantations are mini-towns, usually populated by fewer than one hundred people, incorporated by the commissioners of the county in which they are located. Although Maine's thirty-four plantations have fewer rights than do towns and do not operate under home rule, they are governed in much the same way, with an annual meeting and elected officials called assessors. Monhegan Island is probably the best known of Maine's plantations.

Along with plantations, Maine has three Indian reservations and four hundred unorganized townships. Almost half the state's land area falls in this unique category. These very sparsely populated townships have no local government. They are supervised and taxed directly by the state. Some have regular names—Attean Township, Chain of Ponds Township—but many are identified only by their location on a surveyor's grid: T5 R17 or T3 R12, for example.

Maine's sixteen counties are governed by commissioners who are elected by the people. County budgets are determined by the legislature. In some states, county government is very powerful, but this isn't really true in Maine. Counties are primarily responsible for running jails and sheriffs' departments, and county offices house registries of probate and deeds.

"Democracy is alive and well and living in Maine," says Carole Brand. "Town meetings, church meetings, local meetings are all held and are well attended to decide even the smallest issues . . . should we buy a new fire engine? The whole town weighs in. Should we paint the church steeple? Let's have a congregational meeting to vote. As a result, locals are far better informed about local, state, and national issues, and politicians stay very close to their constituents."

Political Parties

The independent Maine spirit is especially apparent at the voting booth, where people tend to vote their conscience rather than their party affiliation. In the past twenty-five years, Maine has had two independent governors: James Longley, elected in 1974, and Angus S. King, Jr., elected to a first term in 1994 and reelected in 1998 by one of the largest margins in Maine's history.

The newest political development is the legitimization of two additional political parties. Thanks to a recent state law, the Green Independent and Reform parties are now listed on state income tax forms for donations, as well as on voter registration applications. These parties may also join with Maine Democrats and Republicans in presidential primaries and other elections.

HEALTH INSURANCE

In recent years, Maine has had the dubious distinction of being one of the most expensive states in America to buy health insurance.

The crisis started in 1993, when Maine, along with seven other states, passed laws stipulating that no one could be denied health insurance coverage no matter what his or her physical condition. A law limiting the amount an insurance carrier could charge for a health policy was passed at the same time.

The result was that health insurance companies balked at the restrictions and began leaving the state. In 1993 there were more than a dozen carriers in the individual health insurance market, but by 2006, more than 97 percent of the individual policies in Maine were written by one carrier: Anthem Blue Cross Blue Shield. Fewer carriers meant less competition, and less competition led to higher rates for everyone. As the cost of insurance has risen, Medicaid enrollments grew, creating a vicious cycle.

Along with the lack of insurance competition, the state's rural landscape and older population add to the reasons why health care coverage is more costly in Maine.

The Affordable Care Act (ACT) promises some relief. Maine residents who buy midlevel plans in the health insurance marketplace created under the ACT will pay more than the national average, but less than what individuals have paid in the past. While some states will operate their own exchanges, Maine and twenty-six other states have opted to have them run by the federal government.

In 2014, a new consumer-run health insurer, Maine Community Health Options, began selling policies to small businesses, families, and individuals. The private nonprofit is known as a "consumer operated and oriented plan" that will be governed by its policyholders, much like a mutual insurance company. It's one of twelve "co-op" health plans across the country funded under ACT, and its aim is to give Maine consumers an affordable health insurance option, especially those going without health coverage or at risk of losing their coverage.

See the Maine Bureau of Insurance's Web site for more information, as well as a handy chart to compare plans, at maine.gov/pfr/insurance.

TAXES

"Maine's low tax base means a high tax burden," observes Gary Swanson, who moved here with his family from Oakland, California. Most Mainers agree, and various forms of tax reform are in the works. Spending limits for state government and caps on municipal and county tax levies were approved by the legislature in 2006, and a new law enacted by the 125th Legislature in 2012 instituted a Taxpayer Bill of Rights.

With regard to state and local taxes, Mainers shoulder what some consider to be a heavy load, and according to the Tax Foundation, Maine has an above-average income tax burden, the eighth-highest nationwide. The U.S. Commerce Department reports that, in relative terms, Mainers pay the fourth-heaviest property levy in the country, averaging fifty-two dollars in property tax for every one thousand dollars earned.

Several efforts in recent years have softened the tax blow. Maine increased personal exemptions on state income tax, offered property tax breaks to homeowners, and instituted a program that reimburses businesses for property taxes on new equipment. In 2013, Maine lawmakers adopted legislation reducing the rate for the highest income bracket from 8.5 percent to 7.95 percent.

One reason for high local taxes is that traditionally Mainers have balked at consolidation of services on the county model, preferring instead a type of government that is close to the people. However, this means that individual towns are expected to provide a high level of services, including police and fire protection, road maintenance, and public assistance.

Lawmakers in Maine have long tried to reform the tax code (the most recent effort in the spring of 2013) to lower income and property taxes, which many experts say are key to spurring economic development. Those efforts have by and large failed, mainly because they included provisions to raise or expand the sales tax, a prospect which does not sit well with many of the sectors involved. Currently 5.5 percent, Maine's sales tax rate is low—the fifth-lowest in the country—and the state is known for its narrow list of goods and services that are subject to the sales tax at all, but raising it has never been popular.

Of course, tax bites depend on many factors, including income brackets and which taxes are considered. A recent Citizens for Tax Justice analysis suggests that for middle-income Maine people, state and local taxes are actually the same or lower than the national average. Their analysis places greater weight on Maine's progressive income tax structure, which requires wealthy people to pay more here than in other states.

And in another measure of the tax burden, the Tax Foundation estimated that "Tax Freedom Day" in Maine is April 8, the thirteenth earliest in the country. That means Maine taxpayers work until April 8 to pay off their total tax bill. Compare that date to New Hampshire (April 15, the twentieth-latest nationally), and Massachusetts (April 24, fourth-latest nationally).

Finally, tax burdens are relative, depending on your point of reference. Retirees Bill and Allie Lou Richardson, of Islesboro, find Maine's taxes significantly lower than what they paid in New York. Ruth Hohfeld, who moved from California, says she continues to compare her property taxes to California private school fees and feels blessed.

Here's how some of Maine's state taxes break down.

Property Taxes

All real estate and personal property of Maine residents is subject to local and, if authorized by the legislature, state property taxes. Local property taxes, based upon assessed valuation, are assessed, levied, and collected by municipalities. Homestead and veteran's exemption programs, administered by the state, are available to reduce property taxes for those who qualify.

The Homestead Exemption program provides a measure of property tax relief for certain individuals that have owned homestead property in Maine for at least twelve months and make the property they occupy on April 1st their permanent residence. Property owners receive an exemption of $10,000 on the assessed value of their home.

A Veteran exemption of $6,000 is available to those who served during a recognized war period, are sixty-two years or older, are receiving 100 percent disability as a veteran or became 100 percent disabled while serving. Paraplegic veterans who received a federal grant for a specially adapted housing unit may receive a $50,000 exemption. A blind exemption of $4,000 is available to those who are legally blind.

Maine offers a refundable Property Tax Fairness Credit that can be claimed on the Maine Individual Income Tax Form, and a senior citizen property tax credit for volunteer service. A municipality may adopt an ordinance to allow resident homeowners who are at least sixty years of age to earn up to $750 in benefits by volunteering to provide services to the municipality. The municipality may establish procedures and additional standards of eligibility for the program. Because the volunteer benefits are not subject to Maine income tax, Maine adjusted gross income on the Maine individual income tax return may be reduced by the amount of the benefits, up to $750, to the extent included in federal adjusted gross income.

Individual Income Tax

In 2013, Maine lawmakers adopted legislation that consolidated personal income tax brackets and reduced the rate for the highest income bracket from 8.5 percent to 7.95 percent.

Currently tax rates are 6.5 percent and 7.95 percent. The applicable rate depends on taxable income and can be found on the Maine Revenue Web site.

For 2013, the personal exemption amount was $3,900; and standard deduction amounts began at $5,200 for single filers and $10,450 for married joint filers. Additional amounts are allowed for taxpayers over age sixty-five.

Income tax revenues go into the state's general fund.

Corporate Income Tax

Maine imposes an income tax on all entities organized as corporations (except S corporations) that have Maine-source income. The corporate income tax is graduated, with rates ranging from 3.5 percent (for income up to $25,000) to 8.93 percent (for income in excess of $250,000). A number of tax-credit programs have been established to spur investment, including the High Technology Credit, the Research and Development Expense Super Credit, and the Maine Seed Capital/Venture Capital Tax Credits.

Real Estate Transfer Tax

A real estate transfer tax is imposed on both the seller and buyer at the rate of $1.10 per $500 of property, including the value of any mortgage or other encumbrance. Half of the money raised benefits the state's general fund, the rest goes to the county in which the sale occurred.

Real Estate Withholding Tax

Non-Maine residents who sell real property located in Maine are subject to a withholding from the total sale price of the property, to be used as an estimated tax payment toward any Maine tax liability on the gain realized from the sale. The buyer of the property will withhold and remit this money to Maine Revenue Services, and the amount to be withheld is equal to 2.5 percent of the sale price.

Some individuals may be eligible for an exemption or reduction of this payment and can apply using a form submitted at least five business days prior to the closing.

Inheritance and Estate Taxes

There is no inheritance tax in Maine. Maine imposes a tax on estates (gross estate plus prior taxable gifts) valued at $1,000,000 (for deaths from 2006 through 2012) for all decedents with property taxable to Maine. The Maine estate tax is applied even if there is no federal estate tax. For those estates (gross estate plus adjusted taxable gifts plus Maine elective property) with a value equal to or below the taxable threshold (currently $1,000,000) and that have real or tangible personal property in Maine, you may obtain a lien release for that property.

Beginning with 2013, the Maine estate tax has changed significantly. The tax applies to the value of a gross estate (with adjustments for taxable gifts and Maine QTIP property) in excess of $2,000,000. The number of rates has been reduced to three (8 percent on value from $2,000,000 to $5,000,000, 10 percent on value from $5,000,000 to $8,000,000, and 12 percent on value above $8,000,000).

Motor Vehicle Excise Tax

"I do wish that I had known about the vehicle excise tax we pay every year," says Amy Bottomley, who first came to Maine in 2004 for college and now lives in Bethel. It's true that Maine is rare in having an excise tax, which must be paid annually prior to registering your vehicle; however, there is no "road tax" as in other states.

Maine's motor vehicle excise tax is based on the manufacturer's list price of a vehicle including all options, at a rate ranging from 24 mills ($24 per $1,000 in value) for new vehicles down to 4 mills ($4 per $1,000) for older models. The tax base is the purchase price in the original year of title, applying to motor vehicles, aircraft, camper trailers, truck campers, and mobile homes used on public roads. For example, a three-year-old car with a manufacturer's suggested retail price of $19,500 would pay at the 0.0135 mil rate, or $263.25. This tax is paid prior to registering your vehicle every year at your local town office. The town that collects the excise tax can use it as revenue. Monies from this tax go toward the annual town budget and are typically spent on local road maintenance, construction, and repair.

"It is what it is," says Amy Bottomley, "but I do think that the vehicle excise tax encourages people to drive beaters longer. That's fine, but not great for gas mileage or the environment."

Gasoline Excise Tax

Mainers pay a tax of thirty cents a gallon on gasoline and 31.2 cents a gallon on diesel fuel. Monies raised go to the highway and general funds.

Sales Tax

The general sales tax is a flat 5.5 percent, with food and prescription drugs exempt. On lodging and prepared food the tax is 8 percent; on short term auto rentals it is 10 percent.

For more information on all state taxes, call the Maine Revenue Service at 207-626-8475, or see its Web site: maine.gov/revenue.

PROFILE—"A UNIQUE CORNER OF THE WORLD"

Moving back to Maine after graduating from Boston's Emerson College was not something Ben Fowlie had planned to do. After spending several years on the road with his rock band, the founder and executive director of Camden International Film Festival returned to his home state and got down to work, creating what has become one of the top documentary film festivals in the world.

Why Maine? Fowlie cites the state's creative energy as the number-one reason. "The thriving food and art scene make it a truly unique corner of the world to live. We have the amenities of an urban center without the traffic! Your social network is diverse, which results in really stimulating conversations. There's opportunity here in Maine to focus on pursuing what you really want to do." Living here has reawakened Fowlie's sense of the beauty of Maine's environment and the abundance of ways to get outside. "Every time I get to the top of Cameron Mountain, I'm reminded of how lucky I am to have the opportunity to be professionally and personally stimulated by the community that I call home."

3

ECONOMY AND
WORK OPPORTUNITIES

"Just as the Red Sox proved the critics wrong, Maine can compete and can win."

—John Baldacci, former Maine governor
and U.S. representative, from Bangor

What is it like to get a job or start a business in Maine? Clay and Maggy King are massage therapists who came from Atlanta hoping that their new practice would thrive. "We moved here with no hesitation or worries," says Maggy. "I suppose we should have been concerned about making a living here, but we just crossed our fingers and believed that we'd do just fine, and we have." Not everyone has the faith of the Kings, and even they admit it wasn't easy those first few years. "There were times in the beginning that we'd open the appointment book and shake our heads, but those times quickly passed. We were always very optimistic and confident that we'd be okay."

Even if you're retiring here and punching a time card is not in your plans, it's likely you want to know how the state's economy is faring. The answer is a little like the view from Acadia's Cadillac Mountain on a foggy day. It's a little hard to tell.

AN EVOLVING ECONOMY

For hundreds of years, Maine's economic lifeblood pulsed thanks to the state's tremendous natural resources. Fishing, lumbering, farming, trapping, and shipbuilding put supper on the table for Mainers of the eighteenth and nineteenth centuries. In the late 1800s, the Industrial Revolution took hold in Maine, and mills and other manufacturing centers sprung up along the state's mighty waterways and in remote northern towns. Soon shoes, clothes, textiles, paper, and other products were produced in all corners of the state. Fifty years ago, manufacturing was so important here that as many as one out of every two Mainers worked in the industry. In this economy of yesteryear, landing a job in a mill following grammar or high school ensured a fairly decent standard of living and future.

In the second half of the twentieth century, the economic climate began once more to change. In 1969, the industries that formed the backbone of Maine's rural economy—agriculture, forestry, and manufacturing—accounted for one in four Maine jobs. Between the early 1980s and the early 1990s, jobs in this sector fell 14 percent. By 2004, the number of Mainers in those backbone industries had dropped to one in nineteen.

The early 2000s saw the number of jobs in the service industries and retail begin to inch upward. Occupations in health care and social assistance have continued to grow as Maine's economic and demographic picture has changed. According to the state Department of Labor, today these occupations represent more than a fifth of Maine's private-sector jobs.

Keeping the economy strong is a challenge in a state of 1.3 million people living in an area roughly the size of the other five New England states combined. Factors that have had the most impact on Maine's economy in recent years include globalization of the marketplace, development of new technologies, and an aging population.

Weathering Economic Downturns

Recessions, of course, pose special challenges, especially in rural states. The recession that started in 2007 began turning around nationwide in June 2009 (according to the National Bureau of Economic Research) but still has some lingering effects in Maine. While experts say the economy is growing, it's at a slow pace, and the state still has a way to go before it recovers completely.

It's interesting to note that, unlike the nation as a whole, Maine never went a full year without economic growth, even in the worst years of the recession. Between 2008 and 2009, while the national economy shrank 2.28 percent, Maine's economy actually grew 1.11 percent. However, since the U.S. economy has begun to recover, the growth in Maine's gross domestic product has lagged somewhat behind. Why is that?

Charles Colgan, a former state economist and now a public policy professor at the University of Southern Maine, gave a reason during his annual early morning economic talk (aptly named "Breakfast with Charlie") in January of 2014.

"The simplest answer," said Professor Colgan, "is that Maine is not well positioned in the industries that are recovering employment in the U.S."

According to him, Maine isn't expected to recover all the jobs lost following the recession until the end of 2015—eight years after the recession's start. But here's a tweak on that rather gloomy scenario: more Mainers today are working, fewer are living below the poverty threshold, and fewer are dependent on government programs to get by.

More Positive News

Despite facing numerous economic challenges, the state is well placed to pursue new opportunities, and several state institutions are putting forth game plans to seize these opportunities. Initiatives range from innovative education and training programs to meet short-term business needs; to unique regional initiatives focused around themes (think renewable energy, local food, or the creative economy) to long-term tactical investments in research and development to encourage an economy focused on innovation.

In spring of 2013, Mainers received a breath of fresh air when the *Wall Street Journal* quoted Phoenix Marketing International as saying Maine is one of two states that have seen "big turnarounds in their economies."

The *Wall Street Journal* article is based on a new report ranking all fifty states according to the number of people with more than one million dollars in liquid assets counting themselves as residents.

In the latest ranking, Maine has jumped 11 percentage points to twenty-fifth in 2013—one fact among many, say some, which shows Maine is doing a good job in rebuilding its economy from the downturn. The author of the report noted that Maine's progress is especially interesting because the state lies outside of traditional wealth creation centers, such as Boston, New York City, and Washington, D.C.

So—is the Maine economy a glass half-full or half-empty?

Most people associated with the state would answer "half-full." The Maine Economic Growth Council believes that the key to improving economic outcomes is boosting productivity within the state. "This requires investment in Maine's people, beginning in early childhood, and continuing throughout life; investment in the infrastructure that both supports the economy of today and prepares us for the economy of the future, and management of cost structures that impose an undue burden on Maine's people and businesses."

Amy Bottomley, a physical therapist who moved to Maine to attend college and stayed, concurs. "Some of my friends have not been able to find solid jobs in Maine. It's tough for the younger crowd, fresh out of school to find a stable job, unless they are in Greater Portland. I think a big issue for Maine is keeping the younger generations from leaving for greener pastures."

As a mill worker of a previous generation might have said, Maine has "its work cut out for it." But rather than confounding Mainers, these challenges have spurred them to use the Yankee ingenuity and solid work ethic for which they're famous to adapt and begin to thrive in the face of change. Professor Colgan concluded his remarks in 2014 by noting that his outlook was "up," adding, "We are moving away from the crisis and will see steady growth as we prepare for demographic change."

PROFILE—"I FELL IN LOVE WITH THE PLACE"

Ann Harris of Rockland moved to Maine in 2012 from Wyoming. "I have led something of a gypsy life," she says. "I also moved to Maine in 1987 and in 2001, both times from Texas." Ann adds, "I've loved Maine all my life, even before I first visited. I fell in love with the place through descriptions and photos in books. I just seemed to know intuitively that it was my right place." Ann notes that finding good work in Maine can be a challenge, "Especially if you do not know exactly who or what you are. I was a recent graduate—an English major—the first time I moved here, and I landed a job at a corporate law firm that made me miserable, and I left. This last time I moved, I'd become a librarian, and I landed a very nice position. It's important to have some sense of self-definition when you move to a new place, especially a place like Maine that does not have a plethora of ready-made professional jobs."

DOING BUSINESS IN MAINE

To the dismay of many working hard to improve the state's economy, *Forbes* magazine has several times given Maine's business climate low marks, rating it as the worst state for businesses and careers. Needless to say, this finding comes as a surprise to many who are happily making a good living here, so what's behind the negative rank?

It seems our low position is determined primarily by comparatively high business costs relative to the rest of the country. In particular, Maine's energy costs—although similar to other New England states—are high. According to *Measures of Growth in Focus*, a 2013 publication of the Maine Development Foundation, Maine's "reliance on oil and oil products for energy leaves us particularly vulnerable to price spikes." It's not so much the *cost* of oil that comes in to play, but rather Maine's high usage. The report notes that more Mainers (68 percent) heat their homes with oil than the national average (6.2 percent). Becoming less dependent upon oil would give Maine more control over our energy supply and price.

Another factor is Maine's rural character. The state's small population spread over a large area equates to high distribution and transmission costs—again bringing oil and oil products into play. Additionally, Mainers support about three times more road miles per person relative to our neighbors in Connecticut, Massachusetts, and Rhode Island.

Yet on several other economic measures Maine does relatively well. Our unemployment rate is better than the national average and it fluctuates less than the nation as a whole. Our economy, while slow growing, could be seen as more stable.

So just what are the advantages that Maine offers to businesses? Most experts agree that they start with Mainers themselves. Maine's people are dependable, hardworking, and willing to master new skills. Employers praise the state's customized approach in developing programs and training initiatives that meet business demands for a highly skilled, technical workforce.

For instance, in November 2004, T-Mobile USA, Inc. announced their decision to locate their newest Customer Service Center in Oakland, Maine. Although T-Mobile had considered several locations nationwide, Maine was chosen because of the quality of the workforce.

"Our Customer Service employees play a vital role in our company's success," said Sue Nokes, senior vice president of customer service. "That's why we selected Maine. The culture and residents of Maine are very much service oriented, which is a perfect match with T-Mobile's values. This was reinforced in our interactions with state and local government officials throughout the site selection process."

Vitally important to any business is the health of a state's communications network. In Maine, call centers operated by companies such as T-

Mobile, L.L. Bean, Bank of America, and Sitel Corp can be found in every region, and speak to the reliability and capacity of Maine's communications structure. These and many other communications-based businesses are thriving in Maine, and their success is dependent on an advanced, reliable communications system.

Maine was the first state to install a Statewide ATM (Asynchronous Transfer Mode) fiber-optic-based network, allowing efficient digital transmission of voice, data, and full-motion video. Thanks to national communications companies like Time Warner, Verizon Wireless, and T-Mobile, as well as regional and Maine-based companies, businesses here have access to all of the latest cutting-edge services. Wireless, cable, and fiber-optic technologies mean companies here compete globally while enjoying the many natural resources that the state has to offer. In addition, significant investment by large companies such as Oxford Networks, Time Warner Cable, Verizon, AT&T, MCI, and Sprint have made the most advanced voice, data, and video-transmission services available throughout Maine. The state's communications infrastructure is highly advanced—both within its borders and for global connectivity—and Maine's service and reliability ratings are among the best in the country, according to the FCC's service quality data.

The state's location is a boon for international trade, not only because it is coastal, making for easy shipping, but it also borders Canada, an important trading partner. Finally, the state's transportation infrastructure (roads, airports, freight lines, and ports) offers uncrowded, high-quality avenues to quickly move products. Add these advantages to a business climate that fosters risk-taking and entrepreneurial efforts, and you have a winning combination.

Maine offers business incentive programs to help spur new investments; a list of public and private capital funding programs designed to help start-up and expanding businesses; and a growing list of Venture Capital funding sources. (See the state's official Web site for more information at www.maine.gov/portal/business.)

Speaking of funding, how expensive is it to do business in Maine? According to the Milken Institute's 2007 Cost-of-Doing-Business Index (www.milkeninstitute.org) Maine offers the lowest cost of doing business in the Northeast. A decrease in the tax burden and a reduction in electricity cost by more than 40 percentage points when compared to the national average were cited as factors in the report. Maine also ranked well below the national average for industrial and office rent costs.

In the study, Maine was rated the seventeenth most expensive state in which to do business, up from its ranking of nineteenth in 2005. According to the index, Hawaii is the most expensive state in which to do business, and New York, Alaska, Massachusetts, and Connecticut round out the top five.

HEALTH CARE

Health care is a growing industry in Maine, and an increasingly important force in the economy as well. According to the Maine Hospital Association, the health care sector in 2014 represents nearly 106,000 jobs and $4.4 billion in annual payroll, making it the largest segment of the economy in terms of employment and wages. The health care industry has also contributed to job growth in a significant and steady fashion. Since 2000, more net jobs were generated than in all other sectors combined; and barring a slight decline in 2010, employment increased every year for two decades. According to the 2014 Health Occupations Report from the Maine Department of Labor, three things should continue to support strong demand for health services in the coming years: an aging population, heightened attention on preventative care, and technological innovations.

Through a well-designed Web site (www.themha.org) as well as more traditional methods, the Maine Hospital Association's Recruitment Center actively courts health care providers, especially physicians. The center offers the latest information about health care opportunities and provides confidential job searches, all with the aim of attracting top-notch professionals to high-tech hospitals in Maine's pristine, low-key setting.

"Maine's hospitals offer health care professionals a special 'quality of life,'" claims the Web site. "Our hospitals are community focused and committed to ensuring that every patient receives personal attention and high quality care. Hospitals are located in virtually every type of environment in which you'd like to live and work. Maine's famous coastline is dotted with hospitals located a stone's throw from the ocean. Inland hospitals are in communities close to peaceful lakes, fishing, ski resorts, and hiking trails. Our largest medical centers are in small, manageable cities with an urban flavor and plenty of cultural activities." It's true, and many health care providers find the lure irresistible.

Howard Jones practices internal and occupational medicine in the midcoast. "I went online and made a connection with Waldo County

General Hospital in Belfast. They invited me up, and when I arrived it was a beautiful August day. Everything looked like the cover of a *Down East* magazine. I liked both the hospital and the people I met. That winter, my family and I left North Carolina for Maine.

"Those of us in the medical field are fortunate, because we can live just about anywhere and make a decent living," Jones continues. "Practicing medicine in Maine is really nice. You have a different kind of relationship with patients than in other places, because you'll actually see them again in the community. There's a wide cross-section of people, and not very many managed-care companies to put a wall between you and your patients. And I think the people in Maine are hardy, healthy souls."

Other key sectors of Maine's economy include life sciences; renewable energy; aerospace and advanced materials information technology; food, beverage, and agricultural products; pulp, paper, and wood products; marine construction and technology; environmental technology; and hospitality and tourism.

BIOTECHNOLOGY

In recent years, Maine's emerging biotechnology industry has been one of the fastest-growing sectors of the economy, offering more than 650 different products and services to national and international markets. According to the Bioscience Association of Maine, a trade association representing the growing community of biotech companies, more than 4,700 Mainers are employed by bioscience companies, nonprofit and government laboratories, and educational institutions throughout the state. Industries as diverse as aquaculture, diagnostics, immunodiagnostics, marine science, microbiology, and pharmacology are part of this new force in the Maine economy, and its steady growth has been a focus of the state's economic planners.

That focus is paying off. Biotechnology employment in Maine has tripled in the last ten years, with notable nonprofit institutions such as the Foundation for Blood Research and the Maine Medical Center Research Institute joining successful for-profit biomedical businesses such as IDEXX Laboratories, ViroStat, Binaxx, and PharmX. If it all seems like Brave New World, keep in mind that biomedical research and development has actually enjoyed a long and significant history in Maine. The Jackson Laboratory, located in Bar Harbor, is an internationally respected, nonprofit biomedical research institution, founded in 1929. Today, the organization has grown to become the largest mammalian genetics research laboratory in the world. As one of eight Cancer Centers, designated by the National Cancer Institute, the Jackson Laboratory performs research to discover genetic factors related to cancer. The laboratory is also home to a variety of educational programs, ranging from high school internships to a cooperative PhD program with the University of Maine.

In addition to this initiative, Maine has put in place other programs to enhance the future of its bioscience industry. Programs such as the Maine Science and Technology Action Plan and the Science and Technology Report Card initiate and evaluate the application of science and technology on the economy. The Maine Experimental Program to Stimulate Competitive Research (EPSCoR) fosters collaboration between the university system, local business, and the federal government to invest and influence funding in building Maine's research and development infrastructure. Its projects include the Center for Technology-Based Business Development, which promotes technology transfer.

Maine is home to several bioscience and technology incubators, such as the Maine Applied Technology Development Centers, encompassing the new twenty-acre, $2.5 million Thomas M. Teague Biotechnology Center, currently under construction in Fairfield; the Loring Applied Technology Development Center in Limestone, which focuses on forestry and agriculture; and the Center for Environmental Enterprise in South Portland, which focuses on environmental technology. In 2001, the Mount Desert Island Biological Laboratory established the Maine IDeA Network for Biomedical Research Excellence (INBRE), a federally funded partnership with the Jackson Laboratory and ten Maine colleges and universities to increase Maine's competitiveness in attracting federal monies for scientific research. To date, the INBRE program has received $45 million in funding from the National Institutes of Health.

Biotech experts say the main problem facing the Maine biotechnology industry today is a lack of funding. However, the state has increased its research and development funding in an effort to improve the future of its economy and encourage venture capitalists to do the same. Although Maine still falls below the national average in many indicators, current trends mean that Maine is well-positioned to become an industry leader.

NATURAL RESOURCES

Magnificent natural resources have long been the backbone of the state's economy. Fishing, hunting, rafting, skiing, snowmobiling, and forest-based manufacturing industries are all dependent on Maine's woods, waters, and wildlife.

In recent years, fishing, hunting, and wildlife observation produced more than a billion dollars in economic output, supported 17,680 jobs, and generated $67.7 million in state tax revenues.

Although hunting and fishing might spring to mind as Maine's top outdoor industries, wildlife-watching is actually the leader of Maine's recreation industries. In a National Survey conducted by the U.S. Census, 778,000 Americans participated in wildlife-watching in Maine in 2000, compared to 164,000 who hunted and 376,000 who fished. According to chamber of commerce data, nature observers in Maine spend $224.6 million and put 6,020 people to work, generating $111.4 million in wages.

Maine's acres of trees are the basis for the largest manufacturing industry in the state. Forest-based manufacturing (stumpage, harvesting, sawmills, pulp and paper, furniture and fixtures, and other wood products) contributed $5.2 billion in value of shipments to the economy in 2001, or 36 percent of the state's total manufacturing sales. According to the North East State Foresters Association, this industry provides employment for 21,692 people and generates a payroll of over $1.0 billion.

Forest-based recreation and upcountry tourism—hiking the peaks, rafting the rivers—provide employment for more than 12,000 residents and generate payrolls of $145 million. Other revenues from Maine's "Evergreen Empire" include maple syrup (112,000 gallons of the sweet stuff, valued at nearly $1.9 million) wreaths (more than one million valued at $6 million) and over 300 thousand Christmas trees, worth $5.25 million to Maine's economy.

Farming is an old Maine occupation that appeared to be dying out but is now a hip lifestyle choice for some new residents.

"Forget Stephen King and lobster rolls," said Tom Wolf in a July 2013 article in *Modern Farmer.* "The really impressive thing about Maine? Farms are being started at a rate nearly four times faster than the national average, the average age of its farmers is below the national—and rapidly greying—average (and keep in mind Maine is the most geriatric state in the Union), and it boasts one of the highest organic-to-conventional-farm ratios in the United States."

Wolf calls the state "a vital locus of the country's agricultural renaissance," and credits recent legislation to strengthen dairy farming (put in place in 2004) as well as a strong farmer support system. Key to that support is the Maine Organic Farmers and Gardeners Association (MOFGA), the oldest—and largest—state organic association in the United States. Widely known for the annual Common Ground Fair, held in late September in Unity, MOFGA runs training and assistance programs for new and experienced farmers, such as the journeyperson program, as well as apprenticeship and farmer-in-residence programs.

Farmer and photographer Josh Gerritsen advises those thinking of coming to Maine to "have a plan for income during the wintertime. I have lots of friends who struggle when the tourist season ends, but there are plenty of opportunities if you look hard enough, or have an entrepreneurial spirit."

Another important agricultural force is the Maine Farmland Trust, which preserves and expands farmland throughout the state and facilitates the transfer of farmland to young, eager farmers. Since it began in 1999, the Maine Farmland Trust has preserved upwards of twenty-seven thousand acres of Maine farmland.

Newcomers notice the emphasis Mainers place on locally sourced products. "I like buying local, although it gets expensive," says Carolyn Mahler of South Thomaston. "An abundance of fresh seafood, fruits, veggies—all from local growers—and I LOVE the farmers' markets!" The only drawback? "I've gained more than a few pounds eating all of this wonderful food."

TOURISM

Tourism is a traditional Maine industry that is still thriving, despite competition from destinations across the country and even overseas. From small inns to large resorts, trendy restaurants to wharfside lobster pounds, cruise ships to canoe rentals, many Mainers make a good living off vacationers, 70 percent of whom are out-of-staters. In terms of employment, tourism is the largest industry in Maine, with more than 122,000 jobs generated in 2003 and a payroll of $2.6 billion. And many other businesses profit indirectly through the influx of visitors year-round. The state is the biggest beneficiary—tax revenues from tourism in 2003 were $208 million in sales tax, $103 million in personal income tax, and $73 million in gasoline tax.

Can you make a decent living in a seasonal industry such as tourism? That's what Dottie Paradis asked herself before she moved to Maine. "I was expecting a lot more foot traffic," she says of her ice cream parlor in the small inland York County town of Cornish. "I've taken a huge salary cut from what I was making in Massachusetts. But I love running my own business and making my own hours."

Many Mainers agree. "It's difficult at first to adapt to the 'feast or famine' income swings, but eventually you do, and come to enjoy the down time," says Maggy King. Whether your dream is to run a cozy bed-and-breakfast inn or sell handmade decoys, chances are, you can do it in Maine.

BEVY OF SMALL BUSINESSES

The entrepreneurial spirit is alive and well in Maine. Small businesses of all types seem to thrive, with new business activity in 2011 above the United States and New England averages. Nearly 90 percent of Maine companies employ fewer than twenty people, and seventy thousand Mainers describe themselves as self-employed. The state sponsors many initiatives to help small businesses and maintains seven SBDC's, or Small Business Development Centers.

A good source of information, if you are thinking of starting a Maine business, is the state's official Web site at www.maine.gov. Under the "Business" tab, you can access an online Business Answers service. Maine-BusinessWorks, a program of Maine Small Business Development Centers and the Department of Economic and Community Development, can be found on the same site, and provides access to a broad array of business development assistance available throughout the state of Maine, including business education, financing programs, and small business information and assistance. The Business Answers service also answers frequently asked questions. The staff can send you resources, permit applications, and other follow-up information that you need to get your business running in Maine. Also available are customized packets offering information about self-employment, hiring employees, and labor standards, and a Business Start-Up Kit which includes A Guide to Doing Business in Maine.

FAMILY TIES

Maine also has a high percentage of independently owned family businesses. These range from first-generation "mom and pop" operations to sophisticated multigenerational corporations. The Institute for Family-Owned Business at the University of Southern Maine estimates that of the state's businesses, some 90 percent are family owned. Some, like Thos. Moser Cabinetmakers of Auburn, are first-generation businesses owned and run by their founders and family. Others, like the Smiling Cow, a retail store overlooking Camden Harbor, are into their third generation, and an impressive number of Maine businesses go back as many as four or five generations.

United States Senator Susan Collins, herself the child of a multigenerational Maine business (S.W. Collins Lumber Company in Caribou), is a strong advocate for small businesses. She has sponsored bills providing estate-tax relief for family owned businesses and farms. She believes family businesses can be the strongest, because family bonds create a strong commitment to employees and communities that might otherwise be lacking.

MOVING A BUSINESS TO MAINE

A wide range of incentives and benefits are offered to businesses that decide to move to Maine. The Maine Department of Economic and Community Development (DECD) provides comprehensive financial, management, production, marketing, and other technical assistance to help Maine businesses launch and prosper. The department's experts have the broad mission of helping communities and businesses succeed through a variety of programs providing everything from targeted tax relief to community block grants to tourism marketing. DECD and its partners show companies how to benefit from millions of dollars in tax credits, reimbursements, research and development (R&D) credits, capital loans, even direct investment. Check out www.investinmaine.net for more information on Maine's business sectors and development.

The state of Maine is committed to the development of its rural areas with several initiatives. First, the Employee Tax Increment Financing (ETIF) program enables employers hiring at least fifteen new employees over a two-year period to receive a tax reimbursement for a portion of the employees' state withholding tax. The company would receive from 30 to 80 percent reimbursement of the state withholdings for eligible employees. In 2010 alone, the program helped nearly one hundred Maine companies claim $8 million in reimbursements for more than six thousand new, well-paid jobs. Any qualified job creation in an area with 150 percent of the state unemployment rate is eligible for a 75 percent reimbursement. Since all of Maine's high unemployment areas are rural, this initiative benefits companies locating in Maine's rural areas.

In some parts of the state, Maine has established Pine Tree Development Zones to offer additional resources to companies locating in these areas. In a Pine Tree Development Zone, the ETIF program is enhanced to

80 percent reimbursement for eligible employees. Additionally, a company receives a 100 percent corporate income tax credit for the first five years, and a 50 percemt credit for years six through ten.

Maine & Company is a private, nonprofit corporation that provides free and confidential site selection assistance to out-of-state companies considering Maine as a business location. Their services include real estate site searches, data collection and analysis, incentives identification and valuation, and site visit coordination. Mainebiz, a print and online magazine, is an excellent resource for those considering bringing a business to Maine.

What many cite as the biggest incentive for moving a business here are Maine people themselves. Ask just about any employer in the state, and you'll surely hear that the Maine worker is a highly valued asset. Mainers are well known for their strong work ethic and commitment to delivering top-quality work. Labor disputes here are rare—in fact, only one Maine company experienced a work stoppage in recent memory.

In addition, Maine offers a comprehensive workforce-development system should the need to upgrade worker skills arise. When businesses in the state venture into an area that requires new skills among their workers, Maine's community colleges and universities work closely to provide the needed training and education.

THE FINANCE AUTHORITY OF MAINE

Maine's business-finance agency is the Finance Authority of Maine (FAME). FAME supports start-up and expanding businesses by working closely with Maine banks to improve access to capital. It offers a wide array of programs, ranging from traditional loan guarantees for small and large businesses to tax credits for investments in dynamic manufacturing or export-related firms. FAME has also established taxable and tax-exempt bond financing programs that provide loans to creditworthy firms at very favorable rates and terms. Some of the authority's many programs are:

- The Commercial Loan Insurance Program
- Export Financing Services
- Investment Banking Service
- Maine Seed Capital Tax Credit
- Occupational Safety Loan Program
- Plus 1 Computer Loan Program
- Rapid Response Guarantee
- Regional Economic Development Revolving Loan Program

🌲 Small Business and Veterans' Small Business Loan Insurance Program
🌲 Small Enterprise Growth Fund Bond Financing Programs

For more comprehensive information, including eligibility criteria, visit FAME's Web site at www.famemaine.com or call 207-623-3263.

MAINE IN THE GLOBAL MARKETPLACE

According to the Maine Department of Economic and Community Development, Maine businesses are participating in the global marketplace in record numbers, exporting nearly $1.5 billion worth of goods a year. International exports are growing, and Maine is increasing its profile as a trading partner with the Canadian Maritimes.

The Maine International Trade Center offers businesses and organizations international assistance working to expand the state's economy through increased international trade in goods and services and related activities such as trade missions, training programs, and conferences. For more information, check out its Web site at www.mitc.com.

THE CREATIVE ECONOMY

In 2005, the importance of the creative economy was recognized by then-Governor Baldacci, who created a new council charged with advising, supporting, and advancing public and private initiatives building Maine's creative economy. Since then, this emerging sector has been a catalyst for the creation of new jobs in Maine communities.

"People who create jobs want to live in places that have a diverse cultural mix and an innovative and educated workforce," said the former governor. "Maine will be competitive economically if we continue to capitalize on the synergies between entrepreneurship, education, the arts, and quality of life."

Indeed, the creative sector is a major growing factor in Maine's economy, generating an estimated $6.6 billion in cultural tourism dollars. New England and Maine have a higher concentration of creative workers than other parts of the country, artists such as Jane Dahmen, who moved here in 2005.

"Everything we could ever need is here—services, shops, people, culture, etc. I do have my art supplies shipped up from Boston, but it's the perfect place to paint and show work. There are lots of artists living in the area and many galleries." Dahmen says that she and her husband had visited Maine for years before pulling up stakes in Massachusetts. "We wish we had known how much we would like living here because we would have come sooner. Interestingly, we never knew all those years of visiting and sailing here how great it would be to live here."

As an artist, Dahmen is inspired by the beauty she sees all around her. "I've painted landscapes of Maine for years, and yes, the light is different here, probably because there is less pollution. You can really see the stars at night."

The Maine Arts Commission does not specifically help artists relocate to Maine, but they do have a number of services in place for resident artists. Four programs are available: the Individual Artist Fellowship Program, the Traditional Arts Apprenticeship Program, the Maine Artist Roster, and the Maine Artist Registry. There is a formal application process, with paperwork due annually on February 2.

The commission's newest initiative, the Contemporary Artist Development Program, provides reliable information, training, and funding support that responds to the artist's particular discipline, career stage, and professional aspirations.

Maine also supports an innovative "1 percent for art" program, which sets aside an amount equal to 1 percent of the construction budget in a new or renovated public building to purchase original works of art. For further information on funding, residencies, or employment in all disciplines, contact the Maine Arts Commission at 207-287-2750, or visit its Web site at www.mainearts.com.

Entrepreneur Ben Fowlie has advice for those wishing to come to Maine to follow their creative dreams. "Stay committed and stay motivated," he says. "I've seen a lot of friends develop projects over the years that have become very successful. It's something we've all talked about over the past decade, and it's really nice to see perseverance prevail." The other advice Fowlie gives is "Make sure to get out every once in a while. Visit New York, or Los Angeles, or San Francisco, get excited about what's happening out there and bring that energy back to Maine. Perspective is important, especially during the long winter months, and I think it's key to ensuring a healthy lifestyle. I love rediscovering all that Maine has to offer, every time I come home."

LIVING HERE, WORKING ELSEWHERE

With Maine's superior telecommunications system, plus good airports, e-mail, Skype, and next-day delivery services, it's hard to think of a job that can't be done here. Given this same scenario, it's possible to imagine many situations involving folks who live here, but actually service clients somewhere else.

"Neither of us works in Maine," says Jan Njaa, a graphic designer who moved with her family to Belfast. "David's a pilot, and he flies out of Minneapolis, and my clients are still in Chicago. We needed to make sure David would have a fairly easy commute to the airport, and Bangor turns out to be very convenient. I needed access to good Internet service and overnight deliveries for my business. Maine's got it all."

Attorney Dana Strout moved east from Colorado. Although his office is located here, many of his clients are still in the Rocky Mountains. "It's much more profitable for me to work out of state," he says, citing the fact that he can charge more. Although he travels back to Colorado to meet with clients nine or ten times a year, "it's actually less traveling than what I did when I lived there," he says.

Strout's move to Maine in 1994 was, in fact, a homecoming. "I'm a Mainer, and I've got more relatives in Maine than you can shake a stick at." He hadn't lived in the state since his teens and is happy to be back. "The lifestyle and the people here are great. I missed Maine terribly. In Denver, I was robbed ten times in fourteen years. It was time to come home."

THE LARGEST PRIVATE EMPLOYERS IN MAINE

1. Hannaford Bros. Co., Scarborough, 7,001 to 7,500 employees
2. L.L. Bean, Inc., Freeport, 7,001 to 7,500
3. Wal-Mart Stores, Inc., Statewide, 7,001 to 7,500
4. Maine Medical Center, Portland, 6,001 to 6,500
5. Bath Iron Works Corp., Bath, 4,501 to 5,000
6. Eastern Maine Medical Center, Bangor, 3,501 to 4,000
7. TD Bank, Portland, 3,001 to 3,500
8. Central Maine Healthcare Corp., Lewiston, 2,501 to 3,000
9. MaineGeneral Medical Center, Augusta, 2,501 to 3,000
10. Unum, Portland, 2,501 to 3,000
11. Shaw's Supermarkets Inc., Statewide, 2,001
12. Mercy Hospital, Portland, 1,501 to 2,000
13. Verso Paper, Tennessee, 1,501 to 2,000
14. The Aroostook Medical Center, Presque Isle, 1,001 to 1,500
15. Bowdoin College, Brunswick, 1,001 to 1,500

From *Mainebiz*, 2014.

HANDY WEB SITES FOR BUSINESS DEVELOPMENT ASSISTANCE

Invest in Maine	www.investinmaine.net
Venture Capital in Maine	www.famemaine.com
Maine Department of Economic and Community Development	www.maine.gov/decd/
Maine International Trade Center	www.mitc.com
Maine Procurement Technical Assistance Center	www.maineptac.org
Maine Small Business Development Centers	www.mainesbdc.org
Maine & Company	www.maineco.org
Mainebiz: Maine's Business News Source	www.mainebiz.biz

4

HOUSE HUNTING

"I looked along the San Juan Islands and the coast of California, but I couldn't find the palette of green, granite, and dark blue that you can only find in Maine."

—Parker Stevens, actor, former resident of Islesboro

"On the ride to Maine I told my husband not to think about buying anything because I wanted to relax. The first day we stopped at a garage sale where the house was on the market, and the rest is history. We bought our 'summer home' within forty-eight hours of our arrival in Maine that summer."

—Kathleen Hirsch of Owls Head

Maine has a rich mixture of architectural styles and types of dwellings: from grand old sea captain's homes gazing out to the ocean to elegant Federals lining a village square, and from raised ranches with yards strewn with toys to tidy capes tucked into new subdivisions. Picturesque villages shelter lobster shacks stacked high with traps, and comfortable condominiums with water views. You'll find quiet cabins lining lakefronts and cozy apartments topping downtown shops. There are gleaming new retirement villages as well as trailers that have seen better days. And Maine is home to new houses of every imaginable design: contemporary, post and beam, Craftsman, and cottage.

OLDER HOMES ABOUND

Maine has one of the highest homeownership rates in the nation, with nearly three-quarters of all Mainers owning their homes, and many of those homes are historic. Almost 30 percent of Maine's homes were built before 1940, representing tangible ties to the past that few states can match. They are part of a landscape that, in many cases, seems to have changed little over time—proud white Colonials, extravagant Victorians, rambling farmhouses with attached outbuildings and lofty red barns.

According to the Maine Historic Preservation Commission, nearly twelve hundred properties in Maine—many of them private residences—are listed in the National Register of Historic Places. There are 130 historic districts in Maine, each with dozens—or hundreds—of properties. Portland, Castine, Bangor, and Bath all have large historic areas, as do Rockland, Farmington, Norway, Houlton, Belfast, and Thomaston. Even Maine's more remote corners—Chesuncook Village, in Piscataquis County, for instance, a lakeside community that can be reached only by boat—have homes of significant historical importance.

Maine has scores of Federal, Greek Revival, Italianate, Queen Anne, Shingle Style, and Colonial Revival homes, but it also contains large numbers of Post–World War II ranch houses. Architectural historian Kirk Mohney says that most of the state's communities exhibit a variety of styles; however, he notes that the St. John River Valley is unique because of the distinctive early houses built there by Acadian settlers.

The Maine Historic Preservation Commission conducts surveys to identify important historic properties and keeps an extensive library relating to technical preservation matters. Should you fall in love with an old Maine house, the folks at the commission may have some material relating to it, or they may be able to put you in touch with someone who does. And don't forget local historical societies—often fascinating sources of information. For further data on historic homes (or to see if an old Maine house meets the National Register criteria) contact the experts at Maine Historic Preservation Commission, www.maine.gov/mhpc, or call them at 207-287-2132.

THE HOUSING MARKET

Maine real estate is most expensive in the southern part of the state—think Portland or York County—and along the coast, but some pockets inland

and in northern areas are starting to detect a similar trend. Residential real estate prices in the Bangor area had held to a steady course for years, climbing slowly even amid the housing boom in York and Cumberland counties, but this began changing in 2002–2003.

However, rising home values aren't the norm for the entire state. During the last housing boom, prices actually declined in Aroostook County and stabilized in others. The latest recession hit Maine's most rural areas hardest, but gradually these housing markets are showing signs of recovery, too.

Is Maine still a "good deal"? That depends largely on where you look to buy, and what your frame of reference is. Even when Maine's market was at its peak, not everyone saw the top prices as high. Let's face it: for some out-of-state buyers, Maine will always be a bargain.

Raw house lots—those with no improvements—containing up to two acres and located away from the salt water are selling for $35,000 to $50,000, and buyers like Jeff and Cathy Cleaveland, who moved to Maine from Seattle, had to tromp through parcels in several communities before finding their dream property of fifty-plus acres.

What about demand? Even with interest rates beginning to inch upward, realtors around the state say demand for properties of all sorts is growing. Several factors are fueling the gradual increase in prices: historically low interest rates; the trend for baby boomers to "trade up" to nicer homes or to condos; and the expanding second home market.

SEASONAL HOMES

David and Nancy Weil are residents of New York who purchased a vacation home in the midcoast in 2005. Nancy grew up in Presque Isle, attended the University of Maine, and has family in Scarborough and Damariscotta, as well as children at two private schools here. Nevertheless, the couple did their homework and considered several parts of the state before buying.

"We looked at a lot of properties and asked a lot of questions," says David. "It's important to spend as much time as possible in different seasons of the year in the communities you are considering before making a firm commitment, and talk to a lot of people—both year-round residents and summer folk."

People like the Weils have given Maine a higher percentage of seasonal and recreational housing than any other state in the nation. Nearly

16 percent of Maine's housing stock consists of beach cottages, ski retreats, lakeside camps, and hunting lodges that are used by folks who call somewhere else home. For resort towns, these part-timers can be a plus, because they inject money into local economies. The state benefits from the additional sales tax revenue, and municipalities reap more in property taxes without having to pay more for big ticket items such as schools.

The flip side to this seasonal migration can manifest itself in congested streets, overwhelmed merchants, and inflated real estate. Says David Weil, "The downside to living here is that it creates greater awareness of what Maine offers to others and increases the risk that the very special atmosphere and surroundings which attracted us may be diluted over time."

BUILDING A HOME

Home construction in Maine has been rising since 1998, and, now that the economy has recovered, contractors are once again enjoying calendars with few empty slots. Before the "bust," Maine led New England in the rate of housing permit growth, with 40 percent of Maine's construction dollars going toward residential development. While this made builders happy, not everyone was enamored with all of the new growth. Communities around Maine began addressing the specter of sprawl, taking preventative steps to keep their precious open space and the character of their towns.

GrowSmart Maine, an advocacy organization based in Yarmouth, is one group addressing the environmental and economic impact of this issue. Building houses with big yards and long driveways not only threatens the state's natural resources, but pushes up property taxes and makes it difficult for Maine to attract businesses. Their goal is to build a statewide coalition and promote a vision for "smart growth" that calls for focusing growth in town centers on small house lots rather than letting it gallop along willy-nilly. Recently the organization sponsored a major study conducted by the Brookings Institution to look at Maine's economy, cost of government, and patterns of development, today and tomorrow. For more information see their Web site at growsmartmaine.org.

Many newcomers—especially retirees—decide to build houses in Maine, some because they are seeking a special style, others because they desire certain amenities not usually found in older homes, still more because they want to build the dream house with the dream view for which they've long planned. Maine is one of the few places left in the country with reasonably priced shoreland still available.

"It took us twelve years of coming up on weekends from New York to build our house," says Allie Lou Richardson, of Islesboro. "It was worth it, because we wanted to be on the water."

Marlene Kinlin, who moved to Jonesport from Massachusetts, echoes her sentiments: "My husband and I chose Maine for peace of mind as well as the gorgeous, affordable seaside property." The Kinlins retired to Maine and built a home with views of lobster buoys and spruce-topped islands.

When considering a coastal site for your dream home, be sure to check out Maine's shoreland zoning law. This regulation places restrictions on a structure's proximity to a body of water, on the clearing of vegetation near the shore, and on types of buildings that can be located on the immediate coast. More information on the law can be found at any town office.

Consider your new community's architecture when choosing a design for your home. Most of Maine has not yet succumbed to the "McMansion" epidemic wreaking havoc with communities in other states, so if you want people to talk to you at the post office, don't go tearing down a vintage home to build a megahouse. Instead, bring that old gem back to its glory days and bask in the admiration of all your new neighbors. If you buy a vacant lot on an established street (planners encourage this practice, called "infilling," because it helps to prevent sprawl) choose a design and a scale that will fit with the integrity of existing neighborhoods.

CHOOSING A BUILDER

If you decide to build, keep in mind that buying land within the traditional village setting, on established roads, will help keep Maine from succumbing to the suburban sprawl that is eating away at much of the country's rural areas. Whatever style of house you consider, it's wise to take the time necessary to carefully choose your construction team. Mark DeMichele, of Maine Coast Construction in Camden, offers these tips:

- Set aside a minimum of 10 percent of your total budget during the planning stages to give yourself the ability to consider upgrades in materials or compensate for other undetermined costs as the new home takes shape.
- Get the best value for your construction dollar by interviewing architects and builders. Check their financial and client references and look at their past projects and works in progress.

🌲 Choose a "team" that can best assist you in achieving your specific goals within your budget. Remember, the whole process is about working, communicating, and making sound decisions together.

🌲 Another important consideration is your building site. "One formidable surprise that's often found when building in Maine is the condition of and difficulty in developing building sites. Land with the presence of ledge and rock, extreme slopes, poor drainage, and environmentally sensitive issues require more costly solutions for development. Be sure the builder you choose is aware of issues associated with site development and can suggest appropriate steps to surmount specific obstacles."

MANUFACTURED HOUSING

Approximately 13.6 percent of Maine's housing stock is mobile homes, the highest rate in New England. Mobile homes—single and double-wide—have played a big role in Maine's housing growth in the last decade, largely because they are a relatively inexpensive match for the relatively inexpensive landscape. The average price of a new double-wide home (not including the land) was $67,400 in 2010.

Since national standards were developed in 1976, mobile homes have become safer and better built. As a result, loans for mobile homes are available on terms only slightly more expensive than those for site-built homes. New mobile home insurance policies are also available.

Another type of manufactured housing is the modular home. Unlike mobile homes, which are placed on a cement slab, modular homes are built on a poured cement foundation and look similar to stick-built structures. They can be custom built to suit just about any style: Cape Cod, ranch, and even Colonial.

Al Benner, of East Holden, has been in the manufactured-housing business for thirty-four years. He says modular homes are popular—particularly with first-home buyers—because they are affordable and can be readily financed. "A modular home runs about 15 to 20 percent less than a stick-built or traditional house, and they can be constructed in five weeks' time or less," he notes. Quality has improved dramatically over the years, too, says Benner. "Maine was the first state to create a construction code for manufactured housing, which became a model for other states. It used to be that banks didn't want to finance these homes, but as the code has improved, so has the quality."

The Manufactured Housing Association of Maine is a good source of information regarding construction safety, parts, and licensing of mobile and modular home manufacturers, dealers, and mechanics. Visit their Web site at www.mhamaine.com for more information.

RETIREMENT COMMUNITIES

The newest developments on the housing scene are retirement communities. As of March 2000, there were thirty-five privately developed retirement centers in Maine offering living units of various types—cottages, independent apartments, and facilities with assisted-living and long-term-care options. More units are being built all the time.

Located both along the coast and inland, retirement villages offer maintenance-free living and a lively social scene. Many are affiliated with health care providers through which residents can quickly gain access to an entire continuum of care. Retirement communities are set up in several ways. For instance, at Avalon Village, a retirement community on the banks of the Penobscot River only five minutes from Bangor, the home buyer receives a share of stock representing the value of the residence. The equity in your new home belongs to you and your estate. In contrast, Schooner Estates, a retirement community nestled in a country setting near Auburn, offers independent-living apartments, assisted-living studio apartments, and a residential-care living center, but all are rental properties.

CONDOMINIUMS

As Maine continues to recover from the recession, the market for condominiums is once again growing. Given the state's aging population and reputation as a retirement destination, it makes sense that these maintenance-free properties are in demand.

In Portland and other Maine cities, the trend over the last decade has been toward "condo conversions"—the transformation of large private homes or apartment buildings into condominiums. In 1999, there weren't any condo conversions in Portland; two years later, five buildings had been "condo-ized," creating twenty-one condominium units from what had been twenty-five apartments. Today there are scores.

In more rural parts of Maine, condos are rarer than snowstorms in July. "You just don't see that type of housing away from the coast," says a developer in Aroostook County. "This state is still heavily weighted toward traditional home ownership."

APARTMENT AND HOUSE RENTALS

The fact that the heads of three out of every four Maine households own their own homes is a remarkable statistic given the economic slowdown of the early 1990s and our more recent recession. Depending on the community, renting a home or apartment in Maine can be next to impossible. High-growth areas, such as the coast and southern Maine, face a rental deficit that builders and municipal planners are trying to address. In communities where growth is not so rapid, rentals are both available and generally very reasonable.

Renters are in the minority in Maine, and sometimes feel at a disadvantage. "While I've met fabulous landlords here, there are no standardized landlord-tenant rules in Maine," says Dottie Paradis of Cornish. "I've never paid for water or sewer while renting in Massachusetts."

LOOKING AT PROPERTY

Maine is a state of breathtakingly beautiful vistas: mountain ridges that reveal sparkling lakes below; glimpses through the pines of tranquil, rock-lined coves; acres of crimson blueberry fields, stark and austere. It's also a place where, just around the corner, you'll find a neglected trailer with a never-ending yard sale, a dilapidated barn ready to collapse in the next blizzard, or a working gravel pit. When you live here, you realize that conformity isn't what makes Maine special. Whether because of attitude or finances, things aren't "prettied up," and people hold their property rights and individuality close to their hearts. Sometimes out-of-staters look askance at what Laura Read calls "local flavor" and wonder whether any zoning laws apply.

"Readers of *Moving to Maine* should keep in mind that most villages on the coast are still active fishing communities," she says. "I live and work in Kennebunkport. This summer, I had a half-million dollar house on the market in Cape Porpoise. It was a pretty yellow cape with four bedrooms and plenty of yard for kids to run around in. However, to get to it, you had to drive through a lobsterman's yard, full of traps and discarded rope and lumber and buoys and plastic buckets and recycling cars. It took me forever to find a buyer. Everyone loves to eat lobster and to see the boats in the harbor but they don't want evidence of the trade in the back yard. I finally did get a buyer from New Jersey who liked the local flavor and they are happily settled in."

Once you have scoured various communities and pinpointed the areas you like, it's time to find a house-hunting professional to help you look at property.

REAL ESTATE BROKERS

Maine's real estate professionals must be licensed by the Maine Real Estate Commission. Brokers and associate brokers have the most experience and training; sales agents must work under a designated broker.

A good real estate pro is an invaluable asset when moving anywhere. In Maine, they seem to often go above and beyond the call of duty, serving in many instances as a bridge to the new community. "Meeting a superb realtor on our first visit to midcoast Maine was so helpful," says Sonya Arguijo Frederick. "Her immediate friendship provided us the comfort to ask questions and not feel dumb about the question." (Author's shout out to Sonya: thank you!)

Jan Njaa, who moved here from the Midwest, agrees. "Our real estate agent helped us make a smooth transition from Chicago to Maine, and even went the extra mile to show us around once we arrived."

Since a real estate transaction may involve one or more licensees, it's important to know whose interests are represented by each agent. At one time, brokers were understood to represent the seller, and this was true regardless of whether the broker was the listing agent or the selling agent. Today, that's not always the case. The Maine Real Estate Commission gives this advice: buyers and sellers should not assume that an agent is acting on their behalf unless they have contracted with that person to represent them. Maine brokers are required to provide a form which explains the different types of agency relationships allowed in the state, and if you aren't clear who is representing whom, be sure to ask. Here's why: Maine law also provides that a real estate licensee may represent both the buyer and seller in the same transaction (this is called "dual agency") but only with the informed written consent of both parties. Not all agencies practice dual agency, as it creates a real conflict of interest, and may result in a loss of negotiating power for both parties. Bob Fenton, a former broker, puts it this way: "I don't think dual agency makes sense. After all, would you hire a doctor who did podiatry one day and brain surgery the next?"

A better scenario is to find a buyer agent or "buyer's broker," a professional who can help you locate suitable property and acquire it at the most advantageous price and terms. Buyer's brokers can be a real boon to people hoping to relocate to Maine from far away because they're familiar with the local market and can do much of the legwork.

Realtor.com can get you started on your search for your buyer's broker. Find the Web site at realtor.com.

HOME INSPECTIONS

Whether you are interested in a vintage Victorian or a new ranch, a total examination of the house from top to bottom is crucial. Love is blind, so it's a good idea, no matter what the age of the property, to go over the place thoroughly. An experienced and impartial home inspector can give a visual examination of the physical structure and systems of a home, examining the heating system, the interior plumbing and electric system, the roof and visible insulation, walls, ceiling, floors, windows and doors, the foundation, and the basement.

Depending on where you call home, be prepared for some differences in what may be considered "standard" in other places. For example, thanks to Maine's very manageable summer temperatures, very few homes in the Pine Tree State have central air-conditioning. Although some new homes are being built with Southern buyers in mind, it's likely you'll find few—if any—properties in which a flick of a switch generates icy air.

While you won't find cooling systems, be prepared to see several types of heating sources, some of which may be unfamiliar. Maine homes are heated using a variety of methods detailed in the "Heating Your Home" section of this chapter.

Although Maine does not have a termite problem like southern states, carpenter ants can be a nuisance. A professional can check for these and other pests, as well as conduct tests to check for the presence of harmful chemicals, elements, or mold.

Which tests are important in Maine? Drinking water tests should include arsenic (fairly common in Maine's well water) as well as radon, a naturally occurring gas produced by the breakdown of uranium. Testing for radon in the air—a test typically conducted in the house's basement—is also important in this granite-rich state. Released into your home through air and water, radon is a leading cause of lung cancer. Other tests may include mold, lead, and asbestos screening (for homes built prior to 1978) and arsenic-treated wood.

Your real estate professional will know licensed inspectors in the area and can help put you in contact with one. If you can, it's wise to be there while he or she conducts the inspection and see firsthand any problems or concerns. Following the inspection, you'll receive a written report describing the house's condition in more detail than you ever thought possible.

ENERGY AUDITS

A relatively new inspection that is catching on with Maine homebuyers is the energy audit, an assessment that can prove especially important in a state with winters that can be severe. An energy audit helps buyers determine where a house is losing energy (and therefore money!) and how such problems can be corrected to make the home more energy efficient. A professional technician will perform a host of tests, checking for leaks, examining insulation, inspecting the furnace and ductwork, and performing a blower door test to track air infiltration.

It's not just prospective buyers who are signing up for these informative checkups. Homeowners looking to save money and keep their homes healthier are calling energy professionals as well. Speaking from experience, I can say that the audit we had done on our drafty farmhouse was well worth the expense. After having insulation blown in our basement and following the auditor's advice, our home went from chilly to cozy almost immediately.

For more information, see the Web site of Efficiency Maine, an organization dedicated to promoting the efficient and cost-effective use of energy, at www.efficiencymaine.com.

CLOSING COSTS

What does it cost to buy property in Maine? Here is a breakdown of costs to give you an idea.

Bank Charges: Banks require an application fee (approximately $350) to begin processing your mortgage request. This fee is applied to your closing costs, which generally include:

- Loan commitment fee (depending upon the interest rate charged)
- Underwriting fee: $100
- Document preparation fee: $150
- Recording fees (for the mortgage deed): $50
- Settlement fee: $400-$500
- Credit report: $25
- Appraisal: $400
- Flood zone determination: $25

Prepaid Interest: interest from the date of closing to the first day of the next month.

Real Estate Tax: Most Maine communities now use a real estate tax year running from July 1 through June 30. Make sure your contract provides that real estate taxes on the property will be prorated as of the date of closing. Generally, taxes for the current year are paid as part of the closing settlement process, even if some portion of the real estate tax is not yet due. (If a transaction closes before the tax rate for the current year has been established, it is customary to use the previous year's tax figure to do the proration rather than having to make further adjustments once the new tax rate is set. It's a good idea to address this issue in the purchase and sale agreement.)

Attorney's Fees: At closing, purchasers are generally required to provide and pay for a title insurance binder with appropriate endorsements, generally obtained from an attorney. When you apply for financing, the bank will ask whether you want to select your own attorney or have the bank select one.

An attorney selected by the bank represents the bank—not you. Because of this, you may want to select your own attorney to do the title work and to issue title insurance to you and the bank. As long as the attorney selected meets the bank's requirements for liability insurance, you will not be charged any additional amount in connection with the title work. Attorneys' fees vary depending on what is required, but generally a purchaser can expect to pay $500 to $700 in legal costs.

Real Estate Transfer Tax: The state imposes a transfer tax on virtually all transfers of real property. The tax, which is paid by both buyer and seller, is $1.10 per $500, or fractional part thereof, of consideration or value. This tax must be paid at the Registry of Deeds as part of the recording process.

THE TRANSACTION

The process of buying a house in Maine differs from that in many parts of the country, especially out west. Here is a brief overview of the steps involved:

Once you have decided upon your property, your broker will prepare a purchase and sale contract that will include a number of standard clauses as well as some prepared with your specific needs and concerns in mind. Certain types of properties will also require the insertion of specific contract provisions.

For instance, if you are buying a shorefront property, you'll want to require that the seller provide a certificate indicating the condition of the septic system over the past 180 days. Also, you might want to include a clause providing for a review of the purchase-and-sale contract by your attorney before you need to sign.

The purchase and sale contract is not actually a contract until the sellers accept the buyers' offer and sign the agreement themselves. Generally a purchase and sale contract has a number of contingencies. The most frequent are: house inspection, financing, water safety test, survey or lot configuration, and radon testing.

What's the role of the real estate professional during all this give and take? The brokers assist and monitor the activities necessary to fulfill the contingencies and then produce a document indicating when they are fulfilled. Now the buyer's attorney can perform the title examination. The results should be communicated to the buyers at the same time they are communicated to the lender, almost always as a binder for title insurance.

Fifteen or twenty years ago, title insurance in Maine was relatively uncommon and many purchasers and their attorneys didn't bother with owners' policies. Today, though, experts say it's a good idea. Title insurance protects your investment while you own it and also covers any warranty covenants you may offer in a deed to subsequent purchasers. If any of the covered situations arise, the title insurer will either correct the problem or reimburse you for insured losses up to the amount of the policy. You'll also be defended against any lawsuit attacking the title. The cost for title insurance is a one time premium.

Once the title work, appraisal, and other documentation required by the bank is assembled and approved by the underwriting department, the transaction is ready to be closed.

HEATING YOUR HOME

Even the Maine State Housing Authority admits that energy costs are high. "Electricity is expensive here," says Marlene Kinlin, who moved to Jonesport from Massachusetts. The high cost of heating a home is particularly unsettling for those who relocate from outside the Northeast, and many new residents are dismayed to find that natural gas, while now generally available inland, is not an option everywhere.

Far and away the most popular fuel in Maine is oil. "The cheapest thing is Number Two fuel oil," says Willard Wight, whose family has been in the fuel business in the midcoast since 1899. "Everything is on the expensive side—electricity is high, and so is propane. Kerosene, also called K–1, is a more refined oil used in certain types of units, but it's pricey. By far, the most efficient fuel in the state is oil."

Efficient, but at times, expensive. Until recently, the prices New England residents paid for oil had reached near peak levels when a number of conditions coincided to boost demand and limit supplies. Sudden surges of cold weather moving in across New England and much of the Eastern seaboard, as well as shortages of crude oil coming into the Northeast from overseas, combined in years past to shoot retail prices up. (Per gallon rates fluctuate and also vary by region, so check out www.maineoil.com for comparison.)

The issue of Maine's dependence on overseas oil is a much-debated topic, particularly once the snow flies. Most Mainers, some 70 percent, heat their homes with oil, followed by propane at 5 percent, and electricity at 4 percent. The idea of creating an oil reserve for the Northeast is one response to shortages; alternative types of fuel are another.

Natural gas, so popular in much of the country, is slowly becoming more available in Maine, thanks to the mining of the Marcellus Shale beds in nearby New York and Pennsylvania. According to the U.S. Department of Energy, the state currently ranks forty-ninth in the nation in terms of the number of homes (4 percent) heated by natural gas, but that number is expected to grow, and, along with it, a savings for homeowners who make the transition.

While natural gas is relatively rare, woodstoves are a common fixture in most Maine homes. Some households heat solely with wood or wood pellets (and to a lesser extent, coal) while others rely on woodstoves to supplement or back up a primary source of heat. Firewood isn't inexpensive—it usually runs between $150 and $200 a cord—cut, split, and delivered. It can be purchased in longer lengths for significantly less, if you're willing to do the final cutting yourself. How much wood does a woodstove burn in a typical Maine winter? An average homeowner using wood along with another fuel source will burn about two cords. Those using wood alone can expect to burn between four and five cords by the time warmer weather rolls around.

Direct vent heating systems are another way Mainers heat their homes. These convenient, space-saving heaters can be up to 93 percent efficient, are inexpensive to purchase, and are relatively inexpensive to operate. They use outside air for combustion and are fueled with kerosene, #1 oil, LP or natural gas. Common name brands of these heaters include Monitor and Rennai.

Community spirit takes the chill off as well. Michelle and Bill Davis found that "after moving from Georgia, to Maine, it wasn't the cold winters that took our breath away but the warmth and small-town hospitality of the people here. Maine's relaxed pace of life actually allows time to really get to know your neighbors. There's something about being able to walk to dinner and running into a dozen friends and neighbors along the way. That would never happen in a huge metropolis like Atlanta."

RENEWABLE ENERGY

Because of Maine's high dependence on oil, many homeowners find themselves investigating alternative ways to heat their homes, including renewable energy such as solar. With the fast-paced developments in photovoltaic technology and government incentives, some Mainers have taken a shine to this type of clean energy, and panels are slowly cropping up on even the most antique of farmhouses.

Bill Behrens of ReVision Energy, a renewable energy company that has been installing solar energy systems since 2003 in Maine homes, businesses, and municipal buildings, says the forecast for solar is bright.

"Our clients throughout Maine recognize the value of solar as a clean, dependable, and sustainable energy source. Maine receives 30 percent more sun energy than Germany, the most solarized nation in the world. Literally hundreds of homes and businesses here are adopting solar power every year, and the number is growing, because solar is affordable, durable, and ideally suited to our region and climate."

Another renewable energy source that's a good match for Maine—especially at higher altitudes—is a stiff breeze. The first permit granted in the state for a wind farm, at Sugarloaf Mountain, was issued back in 1987, and since that initial gust, wind power has been catching on. In 2013, wind power in Maine generated 7.4 percent of the state's total electricity. At present there are eight operating wind farms, scattered from Rollins Mountain in Penobscot County to the island of Vinalhaven off the coast of Knox County, and another handful of wind projects in the works, including an ambitious effort spearheaded by the University of Maine to install floating offshore wind turbines.

Jeremy Payne, executive director of the Maine Renewable Energy Association, says the state is a "clean energy hub for the Northeast, and New England in particular." Maine's high-quality wind, skilled workforce, and reasonable and predictable regulatory policies are attracting renewable energy companies to Maine, says Payne.

As is the case in other states, wind power is not without controversy. Although polls consistently show Mainers greatly approve of wind power, community opposition has cropped up, expressed as litigation against mountain wind farms and civic activism, especially in the development of municipal ordinances.

Far less controversial is a renewable heating source that is right beneath our feet—geothermal. Acting like a "solar energy management device," a geothermal heat pump takes stored solar energy out of the ground in the winter, and, in the warmer months, stores unwanted solar gain under the property.

Available in Maine since the 1970s, geothermal heating is gaining in popularity. In 2013 it was estimated that more than five hundred Maine homes had geothermal installations, as well as many large commercial and public facilities, such as Knox County Regional Airport. Although the system requires a substantial upfront cost, the Environmental Protection Agency estimates that geothermal systems can save 30 to 70 percent in heating costs and 20 to 50 percent in cooling costs compared to conventional systems.

Efficiency Maine offers a useful tool to help you estimate what your annual heating costs would be using different heating systems. Find it at their Web site, www.efficiencymaine.com.

PROFILE—AN ALMOST MYSTICAL ATTRACTION TO THE STATE

Carolyn Mahler moved to Maine in 2013 from Texas with her husband, Ted. "The cost of living here is fairly high compared to where we came from," she says, adding that she also suffers from "a little bit of withdrawal from not having large department stores close by." But those negatives are outweighed by many positives. "I never get tired of the views—mountains on one side, ocean on the other. And the people are friendly—but not nosey. They are more than happy to help if you ask—and generous to a fault—but they won't butt in." She also finds it refreshing that status symbols don't hold much weight. "You can drive an $80,000 car or a twenty-year-old junker, and no one seems to care."

Carolyn had an almost mystical attraction to the state, years before they made the move. "I don't believe in coincidences," she says. "I don't know why I feel that I'm supposed to be here, I just know that I do. And all the details fell into place very easily. I have a wonderful job and work with an amazing group of people who are now my closest friends. Ted and I are still exploring our new surroundings, and a year later, we are still getting settled. Do I miss our Texas friends and family? You bet. But Facetime is a wonderful thing. Do I miss the Texas heat? Nope! Do I regret moving? Not one bit. This is the way life should be."

5

SETTLING IN

"I write about Maine because it's what I know best, but I also write about Maine because it's the place I love best."

—Stephen King, writer, resident of Bangor

Most new residents find Maine communities surprisingly easy to slide into. "Our neighbors, even in this small coastal community, are friendly, and there's a real willingness to help others," says Carol Doherty-Cox of Port Clyde.

"Maine had a reputation for treating 'people from away' differently," says Ruth Anne Hohfeld of Rockland. "We have found Mainers to be wonderfully welcoming people with little discrimination. People seem to have a deep belief that each person has a right to their 'idea-ahs.' Community is important."

Many new residents are amazed by the investment of time and energy Mainers make in their towns and cities. "I was surprised by the degree to which people are actively involved in the development of the community here," says Kristy Scher, who moved from Los Angeles to the midcoast. "It has been really wonderful and inspiring to see and work with a community of people who are so committed to living in a healthy, happy society. People are much less jaded in Maine—it's refreshing."

"I appreciate the level of involvement available in civic life," echoes Ruth Anne. "The excuse about 'they' doesn't work here. If one doesn't like something, one has to get out there and take action. At the same time, if one takes action, one can effect change."

VOTER REGISTRATION

Voting is an important part of Maine citizenship. Turnout is generally strong, with the state consistently placing in the top five states—and often garnering first place—for voter participation. Presidential election years draw the most Maine voters, with an average of 65.8 percent of citizens casting ballots since 1980. Gubernatorial election years rank second with an average of 52.6 percent since 1978.

Maine is noted for its progressive voting laws. Maine was among the first states to adopt mail-in voter registration (possible up to two weeks before the election), same-day voter registration (bring proof of residence to voting place), and a motor voter program, which permits the Bureau of Motor Vehicles personnel to register voters. Maine law makes absentee ballots easily accessible—just contact your town office or city hall. Maine law also has special provisions to make registering to vote easier for those who have nontraditional residences. Most recently, the Maine Legislature protected the voting rights of stalking victims, by requiring their addresses be kept confidential.

YOUR TOWN OFFICE OR CITY HALL

People in Maine value local services, and pay for them (some think dearly) through local taxes. Nevertheless, your local town or city hall is a convenient source of just about any type of information you need. In addition, clerks at the office can issue landfill permits, birth and death certificates, dog licenses, fishing licenses, hunting licenses, building permits, motor bike permits, and permits for snowmobiles, boats, and ATVs. The town office or city hall is also where you pay your annual automobile excise tax.

DRIVER'S LICENSES

The Maine Bureau of Motor Vehicles (also known as the Division of Motor Vehicles) has offices in thirteen locations across the state where Maine driver's licenses are issued, and offers online services as well. For example, Maine motorists may renew their driver's license or order a duplicate license, renew their vehicle registration, or check on the availability of personalized license plates, all without leaving their laptops. Many other online services are available to businesses, individual motorists, and other customers.

Maine issues digital licenses, which are valid for six years. To obtain one, you'll need to visit the motor vehicle office nearest you (see maine. gov/sos/bmv/locations/ for a complete list) and bring your valid out-of-state license, a certified birth certificate or U.S. Passport, and proof of your physical address in Maine.

Unless you want to brush up on your driving skills, don't worry about studying—written tests are no longer necessary. (A national security check will be performed on your driving record.) You will be required to take an eye test, though, and pay a $40 charge.

VEHICLE REGISTRATION AND INSPECTION

Cars are registered annually on a staggered basis. Generally, registrations expire one year from the month issued. You need evidence of auto insurance (see "Car Insurance," in this chapter) and your annual excise-tax payment to register a car. Registration can be done in person at a BMV office, through the mail (Bureau of Motor Vehicles, Vehicle Services Division, 29 State House Station, Augusta, Maine 04333-0029), and, in some municipalities, online (check maine.gov for a complete list). Most town offices also issue registrations and plates, so check first with your city or town to see if they participate in this program. If you choose to register your car in your new hometown, you may need to pay a small additional service charge, but since you'll have to go to city hall or the town office to pay your automobile excise tax anyway, it's convenient to renew the registration at the same time.

One interesting aspect of motor vehicle registration in Maine is that no notice of expiration or need for renewal is sent. Many a newcomer and old resident alike has sheepishly accepted a summons for driving an unregistered vehicle! The sticker on your license plate tells you when you need to renew, so keep an eye out.

Maine also requires an annual vehicle safety inspection. Most auto repair shops are also licensed inspection stations.

LICENSE PLATES, OR, THE LOBSTERS RETURN

Maine began issuing registration plates in 1905, with the state's first and only slogan "Vacationland" appearing on the plate in 1936. In July of 1987, the first of Maine's famous lobster plates (featuring a single red lobster on a plain white plate) appeared on Maine vehicles, the plan being that they would help promote one of Maine's oldest resources. The crustaceans adorned everything from Cadillacs to Corvettes, until they were discontinued in June of 2000.

At that time a new design, showcasing the black-capped chickadee, Maine's state bird, flew off assembly lines and replaced the old lobsters. But not long after the BMV terminated the production of the old lobster plates, members of the Maine Import-Export Lobster Dealers Association (MIELDA) rallied together in a three-year effort to bring back the lobsters with a brand-new look.

With help from the Maine Lobster Promotion Council, a cleaner, clearer design for a specialty lobster plate was commissioned, and the winning image came from Karan McReynolds, a designer in Rockport. Cars began sporting the new plates in 2003, and by all accounts, the spiffed-up crustaceans are keepers. In addition to the obvious benefits of just having the lobster image on cars all over Maine, the industry receives some of the proceeds from the sale of the plates.

Other specialty license plates honor veterans, the Wabanaki culture, Maine agriculture, and University of Maine graduates, among others. A popular plate features a loon and funds conservation efforts at state parks. The cost is an additional twenty dollars for most specialty models, and five dollars for a veteran plate. Handicapped plates require a completed medical form that can be obtained from the BMV.

Vanity Plates

Vanity plates are available on selected plate types for an additional annual fee of fifteen or twenty-five dollars, depending on the plate. Sally Littlefield of the Oakland House Seaside Resort in Brooksville says the vast numbers of humorous vanity plates on Maine roads is due to the free-thinking nature of Mainers. "We returned from a day trip to Kennebunk-port via I-95, and what fun we had reading the "vanity" license plates on Mainers' vehicles. There is no end to the creativity expressed within the space of seven letters," she says.

"I hastily jotted down some of the more interesting ones spotted on our northbound trip: ALIENS, GO DRGNS, and DA TROLL. This was such fun that when I went to Bangor a few days later I took my time, a piece of paper, and a pencil, ready to take notes. The wealth of creative vehicle registration lettering continued: VISTA, SLUDGE, SWEET-P, TANS VAN, LUNAR 76, MAINAH, B KEEPA (on a farm truck),

BUILD (on a van parked at the local builder's supply store), SNOOP, HEAT IT (on a heating and plumbing truck), OLD BOY, RABIT, BLUE M&M, UH HUH, and DOO WOP."

Sally Littlefield does not attribute these whimsical plates to a dearth of activities during the long winter months, but finds them to be an expression of many residents' characters. "I believe Mainers are creative as a way of life. You have to be a jack-of-all-trades, be resourceful, and inventive when you don't have the right tool to do the job and the hardware store is fifty miles away."

Whatever the reason, you can have fun crafting your unique message on the BMV's online search and order service for vanity license plates, on their Web site at maine.gov/sos/bmv. If nothing else, it's a good way to spend part of a winter afternoon.

DRIVING

Because Maine is a rural state, public transportation is largely limited to big towns and cities. There are no commuter trains or underground subways in Maine. For most people, living in small towns means either walking for services or driving a car. But as newcomers quickly notice, driving about the state is relatively easy and often very pleasant.

"Driving here is much easier," says Lynda Chilton of Camden. "There is no traffic and no sprawling generic suburbs. And Maine drivers are courteous. They stop for pedestrians and rarely honk their horns in anger."

Roads—with the exception of the interstates and U.S. Route 1—are generally lightly traveled and fairly scenic.

A nationwide study released in 1999 reports that the average driver spends eighty-two hours a year in congestion in Los Angeles, seventy-six in the Washington, D.C., area, sixty-nine in Seattle, and sixty-six in Boston. Contrast that with the few minutes or so wait that Maine "traffic" sometimes causes. The only time that Mainers ever have to deal with traffic jams are in the summer in such bottlenecks as the Bath and Wiscasset bridges and at various tollbooths on the Maine Turnpike.

"I have such a hard time driving back in New Jersey now," says Dan Barnstein of Bath. "The gridlock and road rage have only increased since we left five years ago. When people here complain about the traffic on Route 1, I just chuckle. It's so much more pleasant in Maine."

Despite the lack of public mass transit, those needing transportation assistance will find it. Services providing rides for seniors to doctors' offices, clinics, dining centers, government offices, and pharmacies are available even in the quietest communities. In Androscoggin County, for example, Community Concepts, Inc., offers free transportation to medical appointments for qualified residents. The Department of Transportation's Office of Passenger Transportation has a Web site listing public and fixed-route transportation providers by county (explore Maine.org), or check with local town offices for specifics.

Although rural, the state has a free, statewide carpool, vanpool, transit, and bicycling resource for Maine employers called GO MAINE. Dating from 2002, the initiative promotes carpooling and alternative means of transportation and maintains a database of individuals who work in the state and have expressed a desire to commute to work, save money, and reduce our carbon footprint. Register with them at gomaine.org.

AUTOMOBILE LAWS

Maine has some of the toughest laws in the country regarding operating under the influence (OUI). The legal blood alcohol level is low—0.08 percent—roughly equal to one cocktail consumed in an hour. (In some states the blood-alcohol level is 0.10.) And punishment for drivers deemed inebriated is swift and thorough: arrest at the scene, followed by courtroom penalties that include fines and license suspensions. Repeat offenders do jail time and risk losing their vehicle along with their license.

Maine has several new progressive automobile laws as well. Headlights must be on when using windshield wipers. Drivers must stop for pedestrians within any part of a marked crosswalk that is not regulated by a traffic light. Seat belts are mandatory for all occupants in a car. And parents must follow safety precautions for children riding in automobiles. (See chapter 9, "Family Life.")

In 2002, Maine became the first state in the nation to mandate manufacturer responsibility for the removal of toxic mercury from vehicles. The law requires automakers to create a system for removing and safely disposing of the mercury used in cars and trucks.

In 2006, Governor Baldacci signed a bill for a tough new regulation officially titled an "Act to Safeguard Maine Highways," but more commonly known as "Tina's Law" in memory of the victim of a fatal accident on the Maine Turnpike in 2005. The law redefines which drivers are covered by mandatory minimum sentences, creates the crime of aggravated operating after habitual offender revocation, and imposes new penalties.

CAR INSURANCE

The Bureau of Insurance notes that new residents should be aware of the state's financial responsibility law for car insurance. Maine law requires that you buy liability insurance, uninsured motorist, and medical payments coverage. You cannot register your car in Maine without showing proof of insurance. Keep a proof-of-insurance card in your vehicle, too, because if you are ever stopped by a law officer, you will be asked to produce it.

The bureau now offers new online resources for consumers who want to compare auto and homeowners insurance policies. Downloadable copies of policy forms and related documents used by the ten largest insurance companies are available on the bureau's Web site (maine.gov/insurance) under Sample Insurance Policies.

The National Association of Insurance Commissioners recently released two reports showing Maine's average premium for both personal auto and homeowners as the most affordable in New England and among the lowest in the country. The 2010/2011 Auto Insurance Database Report placed Maine third—improving from fifth—in its national ranking of lowest personal auto insurance premiums by state. In the Homeowners Insurance Report, Maine ranked eleventh nationally, the lowest ranking of any of the New England states.

REGISTERING YOUR BOAT

Whether your taste runs to quiet kayaks, speedy J-24 sailboats, or steady fishing boats, there are plenty of ponds, lakes, rivers, and quiet coastal coves to explore. The Maine Department of Inland Fisheries and Wildlife (maine. gov/ifw) in Augusta is the central office for boat registrations and registration records, but many municipal tax collectors or town clerks (and a few businesses) can do the job as well. If you are registering a watercraft at the Augusta office or in a town other than your own, you must first pay your annual excise tax in your town of legal residence. You must show the tax receipt in order to register your watercraft at another location.

Do all watercraft need to be registered? Motorboats of any size and non-motorized boats sixteen feet and over do require registration, and your town office can give you the particulars. Another good source of boating information is the Inland Fisheries and Wildlife Web site, with registration details as well as tips on boating safety, a boating supplies checklist, a list of which ponds and lakes prohibit personal watercraft and motorized boats, and much more.

AIRPORTS

The old Maine joke that "you can't get there from here" just doesn't ring true in this age of jet flight. If driving is not your style, Maine's airports can whisk you off to wherever in the world you desire. Smaller airports offer connecting flights to the state's international terminals as well as the chance to see beautiful scenery from the air. Many communities offer charter flight services as well.

Maine is served by two international airports, in Portland and Bangor, as well as more than 145 FAA-registered regional, municipal, and private facilities located throughout the state.

Incredible as it may seem for travelers accustomed to airport confusion, crowds, and long lines at security screenings, leaving on a jet plane in Maine is a pleasure. Both Portland International Jetport (portlandjetport. org) and Bangor International Airport (flybangor.com) provide true hassle-free flying. Parking is relatively inexpensive and easily available, crowded gates are nonexistent, and personnel are polite and pleasant, not to mention sharp as tacks. Another enjoyable perk: on nine trips out of ten you'll spot someone you know while strolling to the airport lounge. How often does that happen at Logan or JFK?

For a complete list of Maine's airports, along with which carriers they serve, see the Maine Department of Transportation's Web site at explore-maine.org.

FERRIES

Living on an island means working around the arrivals and departures of the ferry. "It can be a challenge to find flights out of Portland that will also mesh with the ferry schedule," says Allie Lou Richardson of Islesboro. "We've become very relaxed about it, and I've found that professionals on the mainland are very understanding when I'm occasionally late."

Coastal Mainers are accustomed to taking ferries, whether for work or play. Private and state-run ferry services provide a vital link to Maine's many island communities, such as Islesboro, and international ferries provide service to Canada from ports in Bar Harbor, Eastport, and Portland.

One of my sons remarked as a toddler that he wanted "to own the ferry that came and got your teeth." Only a child living near an island-dotted coast in an entrepreneurial state could hope to buy out the "tooth ferry!"

Good news for islanders and coastal travelers: in the coming years, speedier ferries will ply the high seas. The addition of new routes is part of an exciting plan by the state's Office of Passenger Transportation to increase the use of alternative transportation. A system of ferries linking coastal towns—from Boston to Eastport and into Canada—is being proposed as an alternative to driving Route 1 during the summer.

More good news came in 2014, when, after a five-year hiatus, ferry service between Portland and Yarmouth, Nova Scotia, resumed. The *Nova Star*, a new 528-foot cruise ship, holds 1,250 passengers and three hundred vehicles, and features a casino, three restaurants, a theater, spa, and art gallery. The ship departs at 8:00 p.m. daily from Portland, arriving in Yarmouth the following day at 7:00 a.m. from May to October.

The Maine State Ferry Service operates most ferries; for general schedule information check the MDOT's Web site (exploremaine.org/ferry) for a link.

BUS SERVICES

Now that buses are smoke-free, they provide a healthy and enjoyable way to travel without having to take the wheel. You can even take in a movie on some routes. The state's extensive bus network includes national intercity lines (Concord Coach Lines and Greyhound), as well as a wide variety of city and regional bus lines providing local and intercity service. Many recreational areas are served by free shuttle bus and trolley services. And four "Explorer" buses operate in key Maine recreational areas, including Mt. Desert Island and Acadia National Park, Sugarloaf Mountain, Ogunquit and Kennebunk, and Bethel. For a complete list, see gomaine.org.

TRAINS

After a thirty-plus-year absence, passenger rail service is back in Maine. Amtrak's Downeaster (amtrakdowneaster.com) provides service from Brunswick to Boston's North Station with stops in between. There's a special late train for Red Sox fans, deals for veterans, kids, and seniors, and the Downeaster Café serves whoopee pies! Amtrak is in the process of upgrading even more existing freight lines to passenger rail standards, and communities as far north as Rockland are looking for ways to get on board as well.

Former Maine Senator George Mitchell got the project on track in 1993 when he sponsored legislation leading Congress to appropriate $39 million for track improvements. Because the initiative involved three states—Maine, Massachusetts, and New Hampshire—and many miles of old tracks, it took years to make Mitchell's dream a reality. But thanks to the perseverance of many dedicated train fans and a joint partnership between the state and Amtrak, riding the rails along the coast became possible once more in 2001.

At the time of the first "All Aboard!" former Governor Angus King said, "The initiative to restore passenger rail service has been in progress for more than ten years, beginning with the largest citizens' petition drive in Maine's history. Ordinary citizens demonstrated an extraordinary belief in the value of rail service in building our economy, reducing automobile emissions in our air, and providing a relaxing and picturesque travel experience to link great locations along the northern New England coast."

BICYCLES

Maine is also actively pursuing bicycle travel, including rails-to-trails programs, bike and pedestrian paths, and bicycle tourism. Brunswick's bike path, which follows the Androscoggin River for two and a half miles, is a huge success, frequented by scores of joggers, walkers, skaters, and yes, cyclists. There's talk of expanding the route to nearby Bath, and some hope it will one day link up with a network of trails that reach as far south as Kittery and as far north as Fort Kent.

Other communities are in the midst of creating bike and pedestrian pathways as well—Bethel, Augusta, and Old Town are just a few. The Department of Transportation has a new Bicycle/Pedestrian Coordinator, whose job it is to work on projects within towns as well as trails that connect communities in regions throughout the state. In the works are three trails—two of which are alongside railroad lines that will again operate—the department hopes to develop within the coming years. Combined, the trails will add up to an impressive 230 or so miles of bicycle routes that will help residents as well as tourists explore Maine from the seat of a bike.

The department provides a list of bike tours currently available in the state, including Maine's route for the "East Coast Greenway," the visionary

"Urban Appalachian Trail" extending over 2,600 miles from Key West, Florida, to Calais on the Maine coast, at its Web site at exploremaine.org. For more Maine bike info, check out the Bicycle Coalition of Maine at bikemaine.org.

One final tip for bicyclists: Maine's Bicycle Safety Act requires operators and passengers of bikes under the age of sixteen to wear helmets.

HEALTH CARE

"What about doctors?" One of the biggest concerns of people moving to Maine is the state and availability of health care. "I wondered about the quality of medical care, especially on the island we'd chosen," says Allie Lou Richardson, who moved to Islesboro from suburban New York. Top-notch professionals and state-of-the-art facilities are important to all newcomers, especially those planning to raise a family or retire here.

Maine continues to offer higher quality hospital care on average than any other state in the country, according to data from the Centers for Medicare and Medicaid Services Hospital Compare Website. Superior care is found throughout the state for two different, yet complementary reasons: first, hospitals and medical practices still offer the kind of personalized care that has vanished in many big cities; and second, Maine's medical community actively recruits and attracts exceptional professionals from other states who are looking for a more relaxed lifestyle.

Statistics from several sources attest to the health of Maine's medical institutions. In 2013, Maine hospitals ranked third best in the country, according to a report from the federal Agency for Healthcare Research and Quality. In 2014, the Leapfrog Group released its Hospital Safety Scores, and, for the second year in a row, Maine hospitals had the highest percentage of top scores in the country, with 74 percent of Maine health care institutions earning A's, making Maine's hospitals the safest in the nation.

What about facilities and equipment? Although hospital costs per case remain less than the national average (and also less than the New England average) Maine's hospitals keep pace with their more expensive cousins in terms of up-to-date equipment and facilities. Administrators credit the state's Certificate of Need law, passed in the mid-1980s, with forcing hospitals to regionalize, promoting efficiency and avoiding duplication of expensive gear.

While the regional approach helps keep costs down, it creates inconvenience for patients when they have to travel forty miles or more for treatments or diagnosis. At times, there's no other option than to get in the car and drive to one of the state's bigger institutions. Although annoying, this narrowing of focus has helped put some places at the forefront in certain specialties.

For instance, Portland's Maine Medical Center is recognized as a national leader in the field of cardiology, with outcomes for heart attack patients among the best in the country. Eastern Maine Medical Center, in Bangor, is another first-rate cardiology hospital, and has a nationally accredited Sleep Center. And the Joint Commission on Accreditation of Health Care Organizations ranks Central Maine Medical Center, in Lewiston, in the top 10 percent of U.S. hospitals. It's hard to believe that a rural state can have such high-quality medical services, but it's true.

And the accolades are not limited to Maine's largest health care institutions. Rural Maine hospitals, such as Miles Memorial Hospital in Damariscotta and Sebasticook Valley Hospital in Pittsfield, consistently rank high in national quality care competitions, another indication of a reality that has been building for years: Maine hospitals collectively are among the best in the country.

PROFILE—A NEW MAINE DOCTOR

Dr. Thomas E. Crosslin III moved to Maine in 2014 with his wife, Ursula, and two young daughters to practice surgery at Rockport's Penobscot Bay Medical Center. Although only in his early thirties, Dr. Crosslin's curriculum vitae glows with accolades and awards, including numerous honors gleaned at Tufts Medical Center in Boston, where he served as administrative chief resident. With the kind of background that could have snagged him a good position anywhere in the country, why did the Tennessee-born surgeon choose Maine?

"The reason we moved here was very simple," he says. "We both grew up in tiny towns, and we know the importance of being raised in (and by) an active, involved community. Practicing surgery here is no different—I have a living investment in the health and well-being of this area, and I am able to derive infinitely more satisfaction from taking care of my neighbors than I would by being a super-specialist in a big city. I had the benefit of being trained in Boston (the best city in the world for medical education), but I wanted to bring a Boston-level surgical skill set to a place I could call 'home.' This part of Maine offers everything I need—from geographic variation and year-round outdoor activities to culinary heterogeneity and easy access to big-city amenities, all combined with the feel of a true small-town community and mutual respect and caring among friends, neighbors, and co-workers. From the first time I visited, Maine seized me at my very core and wouldn't let go. To be perfectly honest, I hope it never does."

EMERGENCY MEDICAL SERVICES

In a vast state, emergency medicine is vital, and in Maine it's improving all the time. Paramedics and emergency medical technicians use the most sophisticated techniques available, and even the smallest of towns boast shiny new ambulances. Training is a constant focus, and even basic first responders are licensed to provide quick, life-saving care, involving the use of equipment like automatic defibrillators, crucial in the event of a heart attack.

Maine uses a unique Statewide Voluntary Trauma System linking hospital facilities with Emergency Medical Services. It's designed to very quickly move an injured person to the most appropriate hospital, no matter in what remote corner the injury may have occurred. And though the state may be rural, the roads tend to be less crammed with traffic, making for quicker emergency transport than in many cities and suburbs.

Maine's "Lifeflight" system, begun in 1998, is a key player in the voluntary Trauma System. Lifeflight's two helicopters have flown hundreds of missions. One of the helicopters' more famous patients was author Stephen King, who was struck by a car while walking on a rural highway during the summer of 1999. The seriously injured writer was taken to Northern Cumberland Memorial Hospital, a small facility in Bridgton, where he was stabilized, and then flown to Central Maine Medical Center in Lewiston. While the best-selling author certainly has the means to choose any facility in the world for his recovery, all of his treatment—including his follow-up and physical therapy—has taken place in Maine.

Knowledge can help in an emergency situation as well. In spring of 2006, former Governor Baldacci unveiled a first-of-its-kind Web site, maine-flu.gov, to provide information on pandemic influenza, also called avian or bird flu. In announcing the Web site, created through a private public partnership between five Maine state agencies and over twenty diverse private sector organizations and associations, the former governor explained, "This means that no matter what your questions or concerns are about flu, or whether you are a physician, parent, or pandemic preparedness planner, this one Web site will provide a place for getting that information."

HOSPITALS

Thirty-seven hospitals serve communities throughout Maine, with sixteen designated as critical access hospitals. Most are private, nonprofit institutions with volunteer boards of directors made up of members of the very populations they serve. This local involvement keeps hospitals responsive to the community and fosters patient-doctor relationships. After all, it's difficult to give impersonal care to a patient whose son snowboards with yours.

Many of Maine's hospitals belong to MaineHealth, a nonprofit integrated health care delivery network. There are also three government-run hospitals in Maine: the Dorothea Dix Psychiatric Center in Bangor, Riverview Psychiatric Center in Augusta, and the Veterans Administration Medical Center in Togus. Maine hospitals have heart: it is the philosophy and practice of the state's institutions that medically necessary health care services should be available to all, regardless of ability to pay. In 2011, Maine hospitals provided more than $416 million of uncompensated, free care.

The small size of Maine's hospitals offers several advantages, one being that treatment often happens more quickly because there aren't as many distractions. When my daughter required emergency care at Penobscot Bay Medical Center in Rockport, a team was working on her before we could even take our jackets off. We knew the doctor on duty, who serves as a Cub Scout leader in town, and were able to call a specialist—another friend—who arrived promptly. While our daughter underwent surgery, my husband and I sat in the hushed waiting room, calm and quiet on a Wednesday night. We felt a rush of emotions, among them gratitude for the speedy, high-quality medical care available to us in our home area.

The state's three tertiary care hospitals are Maine Medical Center in Portland, the largest hospital in northern New England; Eastern Maine Medical Center in Bangor; and Central Maine Medical Center in Lewiston. For a complete list of Maine's hospitals, see themha.org.

MAINE MEDICAL CENTER

Located in the heart of the city, Maine Medical Center serves as a community hospital for the Greater Portland area, as the medical hub for the southern half of the state, and as a center for health research and education for health care professionals. Maine Med includes the Barbara Bush Children's Hospital and Spring Harbor Hospital, a locally owned, not-for-profit mental health resource. Recently, Maine Med was named one of the top one hundred U.S. Cardiovascular Hospitals by HCIA Inc., a national health care information company.

Maine Medical Center is a nonprofit institution dedicated to the highest quality of care possible for all Maine people. It's the state's largest medical center, licensed for 637 beds and employing more than six thousand people. Along with additions to the Children's Hospital, Maine Med recently opened a new inpatient facility for the care of adult cancer patients called The Gibson Pavilion. The hospital has the state's only allopathic medical school (through a partnership with Tufts University School of Medicine) and a world-class biomedical research center, the Maine Medical Center Research Institute.

EASTERN MAINE MEICAL CENTER

Eastern Maine Medical Center (EMMC) is the specialty referral center for the northern two-thirds of Maine. Located on the banks of the Penobscot River since 1892, this 411-bed hospital provides full-service cardiac care, world-class cancer services, adult and pediatric intensive care units, as well as a level-three neonatal intensive care nursery. EMMC is the state's first trauma program verified by the American College of Surgeons, and serves as home base to one of Maine's two LifeFlight medical helicopters—flying more than one thousand missions a year. EMMC's surgical weight loss program was recently awarded the coveted status of Center of Excellence by the American Society for Bariatric Surgery, among the first programs in the country to offer surgical weight loss using robotic surgical techniques. On its three campuses and in its many primary care offices, EMMC provides virtually any specialty medical service

EMMC is the flagship hospital of Eastern Maine Healthcare Systems. The system comprises seven nonprofit hospitals, as well as community and allied health services spread across many hundreds of miles of central, eastern, and northern Maine. Connected by a vast network of clinical and informational technology, these hospitals together provide high-quality, state-of-the-art health services to the residents of the region. Visit emmc. org or emh.org for more information.

CENTRAL MAINE MEDICAL CENTER

Central Maine Medical Center, a 250-bed tertiary medical center in Lewiston, belongs to Central Maine Healthcare (CMHC), a family of health care organizations serving western, central, and coastal Maine. Other members include Bridgton Hospital, Rumford Hospital, Central Maine Medical Center College of Nursing and Health Professions, Central Maine Medical Group, and specialty outreach clinics, such as Central Maine Comprehensive Cancer Center. A key part of cancer care in western Maine is the Patrick Dempsey Center for Cancer Hope and Healing, an organization providing free support, education, outreach, and wellness services to anyone affected by cancer. The center was started by actor and Mainer Patrick Dempsey, and first opened its doors in 2008.

CMHC, together with its member organizations, provides an expansive scope of health care services, health professions training, and clinical research, and is the co-owner of LifeFlight of Maine, with one of the two helicopters based in Lewiston.

COMPLEMENTARY MEDICINE

In addition to traditional medicine, Maine offers a growing array of integrative, nontraditional, and holistic care. Perhaps it is a reflection of the independent nature of Mainers, or their entrepreneurial spirit, but several communities offer a surprising variety of choice in what was once viewed as alternative medicine. Even smaller Maine towns feature wellness centers where treatments in disciplines such as acupuncture, ayurveda, and the ancient Japanese healing art of Reiki can be found, and bigger health care institutions, including the state's largest hospital, Maine Medical Center, have Integrative Medicine physicians on staff whose focus is to practice less invasive, healing-oriented medicine.

Statewide networks of hospice workers help the dying and their families as they go through the physical and emotional hardships of a terminal illness. Homeopathic practitioners and naturopathic doctors across the state treat ailments from allergies to colic using natural substances. Certified nurse midwives and doulas assist in the births of hundreds of healthy babies. And Maine's 450 or so osteopathic physicians are trained and licensed practitioners who embrace a "whole person" approach to medicine that emphasizes the body's ability to heal itself. (Many of these D.O.s are graduates of Maine's medical school, the University of New England College of Osteopathic Medicine in Biddeford.)

NO BUTTS

Unfortunately, Maine has a relatively high rate of smoking. A fifth of adult Mainers smoke, and more than two thousand die each year from the habit. With $811 million in annual health care costs directly caused by smoking (not including costs caused by exposure to secondhand smoke, smoking-caused fires, smokeless tobacco use, or cigar and pipe smoking) the state has targeted tobacco use as a high priority.

Smoking is banned in all Maine restaurants and bars, as well as in all hospitals and public buildings. The newest smoke-free areas in the state will be common areas in state parks and historic sites, including beaches, playgrounds, snack bars, picnic shelters, and enclosed public places or restrooms.

Those less than eighteen years of age are prohibited from purchasing tobacco, with stiff fines for vendors who sell to underage smokers. It's estimated that more than 15 percent of high school students in Maine smoke cigarettes, with another 11 percent using smokeless or spit tobacco.

The Partnership For a Tobacco-Free Maine (PTM) is the Maine State Tobacco Prevention and Control Program. Their Web site (tobaccofree-maine.org) can shed light on Maine's newest smoking rules and regulations. The PTM was originally developed as a result of the tobacco excise tax legislation passed in 1997 that doubled (to $0.74 per pack) the tax. Maine is now one of five states that tax cigarettes at least two dollars a pack.

Although the fight to reduce Maine's dependence on tobacco is still underway, these efforts are not just smoke and mirrors. Since 1998, tobacco consumption in the state has dropped 16 percent, and Maine, which had the nation's highest teen smoking rate (39 percent) back in the 1990s, became in 2006 the first state to win a perfect score from the American Lung Association for its tobacco-fighting efforts. The group measures four categories: anti-tobacco program funding, smoke-free air, cigarette taxes, and youth access. Maine's grades contrasted sharply with those of the United States as a whole, which received mostly F scores in the lung association's annual report card on anti-tobacco progress.

More good news is that sales of cigarettes in Maine continue to drop. In 1997, 101.1 packs per capita were sold, with that number falling to 64.8 in 2006, and 51.1 in 2011. There is much work to be done, but it seems that the Partnership for a Tobacco-Free Maine's initiatives, such as ad campaigns and the Maine Tobacco HelpLine, are starting to make a real difference.

GETTING THE NEWS

Maine has eight daily papers: the *Portland Press Herald*, the *Portland Daily Sun*, the *Bangor Daily News*, the *Kennebec Journal* (Augusta), the *Sun Journal* (Lewiston), the *Journal Tribune* (Biddeford), the *Times Record* (Brunswick), and the Central Maine *Morning Sentinel* (Waterville). In addition, more than forty weeklies cover communities from Caribou to Cutler, serving up local issues and news and offering a good taste of town politics and activities. "Obituaries are amazing to read," says Carole Brand. "Often they are found on the second or third page of the newspaper, not 'buried' (sorry) in the back. They're like reading a life history, complete with hobbies, pets, favorite poems or quotes, and commentary from friends and family."

There's no doubt that reading a good newspaper provides an excellent window into a particular community. Many Mainers also get their news via online sources such as the midcoast's *Penobscot Bay Pilot* (penbaypilot.com).

And what about the big-city papers? Will moving to Maine mean sacrificing forever hard copies of the *Wall Street Journal* or the *New York Times*?

While you can definitely read your favorite paper online, stores in most Maine communities do sell major newspapers such as the *Wall Street Journal*, the *New York Times*, *USA Today*, and the *Boston Globe*. Many local libraries subscribe to these papers as well. The only difference you may notice is that out-of-state papers tend to arrive at newsstands a tad later in the morning than in cities farther south.

Several new magazines dedicated to the Pine Tree State now grace newsstands. Here's a list that includes the freshest and the tried and true:

- 🌲 ***Bangor Metro***. A business, lifestyle, and opinion magazine serving central, coastal, eastern, and northern Maine. Published ten times per year. Visit bangormetro.com.
- 🌲 ***Down East***. "The Magazine of Maine." Published monthly. See downeast.com.

🌲 *Maine* **Magazine**. Featuring creative and passionate people who contribute to the vibrancy of the state. Published monthly. See themainemag.com.

🌲 *Maine Home + Design*. Highlighting residential interiors, furniture, art, and designers. Published monthly, including annual guides. See mainehomedesign.com.

🌲 *Maine Antique Digest*. "The World-wide Marketplace for Americana." Published monthly. See maineantiquedigest.com.

🌲 *MaineBiz*. Maine's premier statewide business news publication. Published every other week. See mainebiz.biz.

🌲 *Maine Boats, Homes and Harbors*. Published five times a year. Visit the Web site at maineboats.com.

🌲 *Maine Seniors*. Focusing on golden-aged Mainers. Published monthly. Contact meseniors.com.

🌲 *Old Port Magazine*. A new quarterly focusing on Portland's peninsula. Published four times per year.

🌲 *Portland Magazine*. Highlighting the vibrancy of Portland and published monthly. Visit portlandmonthly.com.

SHOPPING

In an era in which shopping is ranked one of America's favorite activities, it comes as no surprise that some newcomers cite lack of retail choice as one of the biggest challenges to living in Maine. Indoor malls are few: the Maine Mall in South Portland, the Bangor Mall, the Auburn Mall, and the Aroostook Mall in Presque Isle. While Freeport, with its village of stores; Augusta, with two clusters of shopping areas; and Kittery, with dozens of outlet shops, are shopping destinations, in most communities smaller stores offering more personal service are the norm.

"Shopping has been my biggest challenge," admits Lynda Chilton of Camden. "Here in the midcoast we are at least an hour's drive from any mall or large department store. So trips for clothing, shoes, and specialty items which were only fifteen minutes away in Virginia have required some new strategies here. We have had to slow down our expectations, which is not necessarily a bad thing."

New residents have different ways of adapting to the dearth of large department stores. Some take shopping trips to busier areas once in a while. Others rely on catalogs or the Internet for purchases. After all, the growth of catalog and online retailing means miles don't matter—you can shop wherever and whenever. (UPS, Federal Express, and Airborne all make regular deliveries, and no extra time is required.) Some folks are pleasantly surprised to find they can live a little more simply in Maine, where consumerism is not a competitive sport. In other words, they buy less.

Of course, not everyone thinks the scarcity of sprawling malls is a hardship. Most people here—newcomers included—far prefer spruces to strip malls, not regretting the absence of the traffic, chain stores, noise, and bustle for which shopping areas have become known. "Readers considering relocation should know that there isn't a mall around the corner and that most of us love it that the stores are often closed on holidays," says Ruth Anne Hohfeld. And many come to cherish the kind of personal service smaller shops offer, service that is unavailable in busy big-box retailers. They appreciate the service from booksellers like Maine Coast Books in Damariscotta, for instance, where the owner knows just what type of mystery you enjoy. Or hardware stores like Rankins, in Camden, where third-generation-owner Lisa Rankin Burgess points you personally toward the right hinge. Service, attention, courtesy, and quality—these are the commonplace little things that make shopping a pleasure in Maine's small stores.

ALCOHOL SALES

While many of us today are partial to a cup of coffee during the working day, Mainers of the early nineteenth century were far more likely to take "rum breaks." Back then, Maine was a major player in the seagoing "triangle trade" to the West Indies, with "demon rum" a profitable cargo in many a schooner's hold.

Despite (or perhaps because of) this fondness for rum, Maine was the first state to pass laws banning alcoholic beverages, earning it the title, "Birthplace of Prohibition." Temperance may have been popular with some, but others frequented their local bootlegger. More daring were smugglers who made clandestine trips to Canada, rum runners in their sloops, and bands of liquor pirates who raided them.

That exacting era ended with the repeal of Prohibition in the 1930s. Or did it? Some Maine communities rejected the return of legal spirits, and to this day more than forty communities in the state have some type of restriction on alcohol sales.

Outside of these communities, anyone over the age of twenty-one wishing to buy some bubbly can find it readily at privately owned "agency stores." These establishments are located within larger supermarkets or convenience stores. Liquor prices are strictly regulated and are higher than in neighboring New Hampshire and Canada, which leads many people to stock up before crossing into Maine. To compete, the state-owned stores in Kittery and Calais offer discount prices—as much as 10 percent lower than the rest of the state.

MAINE BEER, WINE, AND SPIRITS

Speaking of adult beverages, Maine is becoming increasingly well known for the excellence of its craft brewing and high-quality spirit producers. From The Shipyard Brewing Company, hand-crafting award-winning beer in Maine for nearly twenty years (and now one of the largest craft breweries in the country) to Cold River Vodka, a family business where gin and vodka made from Maine potatoes is triple-distilled in copper pots, there are dedicated producers here who are becoming nationally recognized. Maine is surprisingly fertile territory for growing grapes, too, and wineries large and small are popping up in every corner of the state. You can follow one of three Maine Wine Trails, meandering from Lincolnville's Cellardoor Winery through the rolling hills to Two Hogs Winery in Vassalboro, and everywhere in between. One good way to sip and savor is to participate in Open Winery Day, held annually in June and sponsored by the Maine Winery Guild, or any of the state's festivals and fairs highlighting locally produced beer and spirits, such as Portland's Harvest on the Harbor.

MAINE CUISINE

Another tasty benefit of life in Maine is the freshness and variety of great things to eat. In many parts of the state, food ranges from the simple to the sophisticated, from nouveau cuisine to nostalgic favorites. Restaurants with creative chefs offer new twists on local ingredients like fiddlehead ferns or smoked mussels, as well as more traditional fare that changes with the seasons. Ethnic cuisine—once scarce in the state—is increasingly common, even in many small towns, and locally sourced ingredients are more and more the rule. Maine producers find there's a real demand for all kinds of things hailing from the state—in a survey done in 2014, four out of five Mainers said they prefer eating locally raised products.

The state has its share of nationally recognized restaurants, too—almost too many to count—as well as newcomers on the scene such as Portland's Fisherman's Grill, which placed first in a 2014 Yelp ranking of New England's best seafood spots, or Camden's Long Grain, named as a favorite in a 2013 article in *The Guardian*. There are James Beard award-winning chefs and semifinalists here, too, and they aren't just simmering their signature dishes in the state's urban areas.

Along with the old standbys such as diners, lobster shacks, and family eateries where generations of Maine residents and tourists have shared a meal, new restaurants are firing up their grills all the time. Nevertheless, some newcomers compare menus from large metropolitan areas outside of the state and come up—well, a little hungry.

"There are two extremes of restaurants in Maine, and very few in betweeners," says Carole Brand. "The first is represented by Moody's Diner—a Maine tradition from the early 1900s where the menu has not changed since the opening (although the prices have), every item on the menu qualifies as 'comfort food' (think macaroni and cheese and chocolate chiffon pie), and the concept of low carb must apply to your car engine and not your diet. The second is an astonishingly sophisticated and high-end restaurant like Primo in Rockland, where reservations are required weeks in advance (months in the summer), presentation is as important as palate, and the menu contains items you are not comfortable pronouncing let alone eating . . . but what you do eat is exquisite. Both varieties of restaurants have their passionate aficionados and long waiting lines."

Nancy Lawson moved to Maine in 2004 from California and says she finds "a lack of restaurants—especially Mexican restaurants—that offer good food at a good price." Ruth Anne Hohfeld, also an ex-Californian, thinks newcomers should know that "potlucks are better than most of the restaurants and much more fun."

Ruth Anne has a point: casual dinners in which everyone brings a dish are popular in Maine, as are bean suppers, chicken dinners, and the famous big-clawed crustacean, *Homarus Americanus*.

To say that Maine is internationally known for lobster (more than forty-six million pounds of the stuff are harvested in a typical year) is an understatement. Maine is practically synonymous with the King of Seafood, and when you live here, you find yourself serving it to satisfied guests quite often. The Gulf of Maine is home to other equally delicious (although not as famous) gifts from the sea, such as mussels, clams, shrimp, scallops, and fish of all stripes. Some varieties you can catch yourself—others can be found at local supermarkets, fish markets, or fresh at the dock.

When selecting your next lobster, consider this advice from the Maine Lobster Promotion Council (mainelobsterpromo.com/index.html):

- **Color**: Maine lobsters are usually greenish brown or black in color, but can also be blue, yellow, red, or even white. The color of a lobster's shell does not affect its flavor or texture.
- **Activity**: Look for lobsters that move around and hold their claws upward and their tails straight. Claws should never hang limply and the tail should never curl underneath the body.
- **Shells**: Black marks or holes in the lobster's shell are the result of wear and tear and usually indicate an older lobster that hasn't recently shed its shell. Marks are not harmful in any way.
- **Hard Shell Lobster**: Hard shell lobsters have been living in their shells for quite a while, and so they're usually fuller. However, it requires the use of utensils to gain access to the meat.
- **New Shell Lobster**: New shell lobsters have recently molted and are growing into their new shells. Many people think new shell lobster meat is sweeter and more tender than the meat of a hard shell lobster and it is significantly easier to remove from the shell.

If seafood's not your style, markets and restaurants offer just about anything you crave—certified Black Angus beef, organically raised chickens, free-range turkeys, and spring lamb are just a few delicious possibilities. Small farms supply fresh eggs as well as a tempting array of cheeses, vegetables, and fruits. Farmers' markets display items like crunchy greens, fresh corn, and maple syrup, and supermarkets provide a wide variety of local (as well as imported) products and produce.

One item you may see on a Maine menu is the famous "Italian," a sandwich that combines ham, American cheese, and fresh veggies on a soft roll. The restaurant that brought the item to fame is Amato's, but you'll find the popular sandwich at pizza parlors and lunch counters throughout the state.

The changing seasons bring more of Maine's bounty: strawberries, raspberries, cranberries, and tangy little blueberries that thrive in our acidic soil. Come July, it's easy to see why the state produces 98 percent of the country's lowbush blueberries. Apples are another significant crop. Heirloom varieties like tart Northern Spies ripen alongside more common varieties such as Macintosh and Delicious at orchards large and small.

Living in Maine means savoring a whole pantry of delicious foods, including our famous red crustaceans, and hosting your share of potlucks.

"I can eat a lobster roll for lunch," says Gloria Guiduli, who moved to the midcoast from Massachusetts in 2000. "Or sushi at the Japanese place, wonderful Italian food, and fresh croissants just out of the oven. Before I moved up, I wondered if finding ingredients for recipes here would be difficult, but I'm able to locate what I need at the local supermarkets and specialty stores."

PROFILE—A TRANSPLANT FROM THE BIG CITY

"I should have prepared myself more for the lack of retail therapy," says Sonya Arguijo Frederick, who moved to Maine with her husband Erik and four small children in 2013. "I didn't really think about the differences between the big city and the Maine lifestyle, and I could have spent more time preparing myself." With that said, Sonya says she is enjoying the things that make Maine special. "Hands down, it's the beauty of the natural surroundings," she says. "I am constantly awestruck by the postcard views at every corner. I truly believe that the beauty outside every window has brought me closer to God. My favorite view is when the ice and snow have blanketed the trees and ground. The glistening of the snow is like diamonds all around. I like to think of them as little angels flapping their wings." Another pleasant surprise? "Dogs are people in Maine. They are invited to go with you ANYWHERE."

6

WEATHER AND WILDLIFE

"The coldest winter I ever spent was a summer in Maine."

—Mark Twain

Summers in Maine are exquisite. Despite what Mr. Twain may have quipped, the state boasts one of the most comfortable summer climates in the continental United States, a prime reason why thousands of vacationers started "summering" here in the first place. And autumn is nothing short of glorious, with the crimsons and golds of the changing foliage enhanced by sunny, dry days in the sixties and low seventies.

And then there's winter. Most of the country harbors exaggerated notions about the severity of Maine's weather come December. Even southern New Englanders believe Old Man Winter saves the full force of his wrath for the Pine Tree State, relentlessly dumping foot after foot of the white stuff on uncomplaining Mainers. And springtime?

"Two words," says transplant Barry Hurtt, a mid-westerner who moved to Rockland. "Mud season."

A FOUR-SEASON CLIMATE

This part of the country has four distinct seasons, and that in itself can be a challenge for newcomers accustomed to the same weather no matter what the calendar reads. "I was concerned before moving about dealing with a truly seasonal climate," admits Gary Swanson, who moved with his family to Rockland from the West Coast. "Coming from California, we've found the weather associated with each of Maine's seasons to be quite dramatic. But if you're prepared, it's really a very livable climate."

Carole Brand agrees. "Frankly, I think the weather is an advantage. The summers are cool and the winters are manageable." Carole had wondered whether the winters would "live up to their reputation," but she says "good snow removal, road maintenance, weather reports, and a gas fireplace make winter not a problem."

There are many good-natured jokes about Maine's seasons, and in particular, their length and arrival dates. People quip that summer hits on the Fourth of July and winter sets in on July 5. Others maintain that "black fly season" comes with the melting snow, and that autumn is announced not by crisp, cool days, but by the onslaught of the fall tourists, or "leaf peepers."

My favorite definition of Maine's meteorological year is that it's "nine months of winter, and three months of mighty rough sleddin'."

But in reality, the climate is generally more moderate (especially along the coast) than in other northern states. Maine's size and its varied topography can make the weather very different in each corner of the state at any given time. Coastal areas receive cool breezes in the summer and warmer air in the winter. When it snows in the western mountains, it may rain Down East and be sunny on the south coast. Kids in Caribou do a great deal more sledding than do their counterparts in Kennebunkport.

Winter

"Before I moved here, I wondered, 'What are the winters really like?'" says Barry Hurtt. "But after a decade in Chicago, Maine winters are no big deal."

Anyone accustomed to winters like those dished out in the Midwest can take Maine weather in stride. Contrary to popular belief, winter begins on the late side—some years, not until mid-December. It's generally cold here, ranging between 21 degrees and 32 degrees in January, depending on where you are, but prolonged cold spells of several weeks are rare. Average snowfall ranges from 50 to 110 inches—again, depending on where you are when the flakes fly.

Folks who aren't used to chilly temperatures are often surprised that life goes on even when the mercury drops a little. "We were amazed to see how active everyone is in the winter," says Thad Chilton of Camden. "It's great to see families out walking, skiing, and having a good time together." And people who have spent several winters often grow to appreciate the profound beauty of the countryside under a blanket of white and the moody light and colors of the boreal sky.

That's not to say a mean winter can't pack a punch or two. "I wish I hadn't underestimated how brutal Maine winters can be!" says Josh Gerritsen, who moved back to Maine in 2012. "I was wholly unprepared for winter last year." Despite the record-breaking snows of 2014, old-timers claim that today's storms are considerably tamer than the legendary blizzards of yore. "Winter is our most variable season," says Gregory Zielinski, state climatologist and University of Maine professor. "Some are cold, some are warm." Zielinski says Maine winters have a tendency to run on ten- to twenty-year cycles. "The 1950s to the 1970s, we had more cold and snowy winters than not," he says. "In the late 1970s, 1980s, and part of the 1990s, we had more warmer and less snowy winters."

This propensity is the result of the rapport between a low pressure system near Iceland and a high pressure system near the Azores, called the North Atlantic oscillation. Pressure differences in the Atlantic Ocean affect the form of the jet stream—fast-moving winds that blow west to east at high altitudes—which in turn influences much of Maine's weather.

Even in a mild year, the occasional northeaster may drop several inches, prompting television weathermen to put on their sweaters and predict doom and school superintendents to cancel classes. But there is not as much fanfare as you might think. Perhaps because Maine is a state adept at dealing with the white stuff, people often view winter storms more as an occasional treat than a frequent and daunting threat.

"While it snows more heavily and more often in Maine than in New Jersey, Maine snow has apparently acquired the ability to disappear within twenty-four hours after falling," says Carole Brand. "It is a mystery where it goes . . . but the day after a snowstorm, not only are the roads and shoulders perfectly clear and dry, but the streets and sidewalks in town are also completely empty and passable. No enormous snowbanks to hurdle; no walking blocks to find a path shoveled through the snow; I'm not even sure why I bought a new pair of boots. I have a feeling there is a Maine Snow Depository where the towns deposit the shoveled snow and those in the know can go skiing in August."

Many towns do have an ordinance that the streets must be clear within twenty-four hours of a snowfall. "I've been impressed with how well maintained Maine roads are in the winter," notes Allie Lou Richardson of Islesboro. "Crews are at the ready to deal with storms right away."

Elizabeth Burrell of Rockland, a veteran of several Maine winters, agrees. "Don't worry about the weather," she advises. "Towns here are really very well adapted to dealing with whatever comes up."

PROFILE—A NEW MAINER'S FIRST WINTER

The winter of 2013–2014 was one of the coldest to hit Maine in decades, and it was Floridian Nan Rowe's very first. "The snow and cold I was okay with," she says. "My biggest challenge was the darkness, especially when dusk came at four p.m. in December!" Rowe, who purchased an equestrian property in rural Searsmont, says that although the darkness did not depress her, "I wasn't crazy about it. On the flip side, I was pleasantly surprised to find that before the month of January was up, we'd gained a whole hour more of daylight." With a chuckle Rowe says the plethora of bright bulbs twinkling during December's dark days—even in the most remote corners of Maine—serve a real purpose. "Now I know why the whole state lights up like a Christmas tree," she jokes.

WILDLIFE

Maine is home to a vast array of wildlife—one of the most varied populations in the eastern United States, in fact. White-tailed deer, bobcats, black bears, coyotes, loons, seals, osprey, chipmunks, raccoons, beavers, lynx, muskrats, squirrels, otters, foxes, minks, weasels, skunks, and porcupines—the list goes on and on, including threatened species such as bald eagles, Blanding's turtles, and puffins, those colorful "sea parrots" that are making a comeback along the Maine coast. Most famous of all of the state's animals is probably its largest—the moose. "One advantage to moving here," quips Marlene Kinlin of Jonesport, "is watching moose stroll through my front yard."

It isn't every day that a moose comes to call, but living in Maine does make it possible. After all, there are more than sixty thousand of the big beasts in the state. Their footprints are often visible on muddy hiking trails or dirt roads, and their spreading antlers adorn many a fireplace mantel. Given a little luck and a kayak, you can paddle to a quiet cove on Moosehead Lake and spy one munching aquatic weeds—a favorite treat. On rare occasions, moose will even venture into busy downtown areas (we had one clip-clopping down our street one spring) or stroll across golf courses.

Rarer by far are sightings of wolves and mountain lions, two recent additions to Maine's endangered species list. Although state biologists have long questioned their existence here, both of these predators are found in

Canada, and reports of their presence in Maine persist. In June 2000, a wolf-like animal was captured west of Baxter State Park but managed to escape before DNA testing could be done on it. An animal believed to be a wolf was trapped in Aurora in 1996, but genetic testing later indicated it to be a wolf hybrid.

"We believe very strongly that wolves are here," said John Glowa, founder and leader of the Maine Wolf Coalition, in a January 2014 article in the *Bangor Daily News*. The animals have been documented in Massachusetts and New York, he noted, as well as Quebec and New Brunswick. Maine contains "tens of thousands of square miles, much of it suitable for wolf habitat."

Wolf experts from Wisconsin performed an assessment here in 2011 and agreed that the state has large areas of suitable wolf habitat and could support a fairly large population of the canines; however, they found no evidence that wolves were successfully dispersing here.

Maine is home to Canada lynx and bobcats, but for years biologists said that any actual mountain lions that lived in Maine were likely former pets that had been released into the wild. In 2011 that theory took a catnap when a mountain lion was struck by a car in southern New England. DNA testing determined the dead cougar had been previously documented in South Dakota. At that point, biologists conceded that a roaming mountain lion could probably slink its way into Maine. The interlopers would be solitary and seeking mates in a state that would have precious few options. The biologists concluded that therefore the chance of an actual breeding population of the big cats here in Maine is still very, very small.

Large predators notwithstanding, it's a relief to discover that Maine lacks many of the poisonous critters that plague other states, although we do have a problem with ticks and Lyme disease, discussed later in this chapter. Luckily, there are no poisonous snakes to contend with, no scorpions, and very few venomous insects. Instead, more than 150 insects in the order *Odonata*, damselflies and dragonflies, flit on translucent wings over ponds, bogs, and fields. Nonpoisonous and colorful, they are a significant and conspicuous component of Maine's wildlife diversity.

One of new resident Nan Rowe's biggest surprises was another type of insect that she hadn't seen since childhood: the firefly, a winged beetle in the family *Lampyridae*.

"The first time I walked out to my backyard and saw the yellow-green flashes of light, I almost cried," she says. "I hadn't seen fireflies since I was a little girl, visiting my grandparents in Wisconsin, and I'd figured they were all gone."

Perhaps these little "lightning bugs" are missing from much of the country, but happily they are alive and well, illuminating summer nights in towns across Maine.

"Having lived in various versions of suburbia up until my move here," Rowe says, "I can't tell you how magical it was to see that not everything has fallen by the wayside."

Birding

Maine's diversity of coastal and inland habitats offers birders the chance to add lots of feathered friends to their life list—more than 450 species have been identified in the state. In addition to the cheerful little black-capped chickadee, whose two-note song is such a harbinger of spring, there are robins and other thrushes, killdeer, bluejays, gray jays, starlings, crows, phoebes, kingfishers, common grackles, and warblers. Grosbeaks, crossbills, sparrows, and other finches commonly nest in Maine's woodlands, meadows, and swamps. Predatory birds found in Maine include owls and hawks, such as ospreys and red-tailed hawks, and bald eagles. Maine is the nesting and breeding ground for numerous migrant species of coastal and inland birds and offers the opportunity to see rare and beautiful species like puffins and loons. In fact, Maine is fortunate to have the largest population of loons in all of New England, estimated at four thousand adults. Since 1977, Maine Audubon Society has been working to protect the common loon in Maine, and thanks to their vigilance, the loon population now seems fairly stable.

For a checklist of Maine birds, see the Audubon Society's Web site at maineaudubon.org. Another good Web site for bird identification, sites, and trips is mainebirdingtrail.com.

Faces from the Past

Currently thirty-four species of fish and wildlife are listed as endangered or threatened under Maine's Endangered Species Act. Some are also listed on the federal government's list.

The state's Department of Inland Fisheries and Wildlife (MDIFW) is working with concerned citizens and other groups to boost the dwindling numbers of animals such as piping plovers, box turtles, and twilight moths, and hopefully these efforts will succeed. Some species, like the peregrine falcon, have already shown great progress thanks in large part to protection of nesting sites. (Acadia National Park closes two popular hiking trails dur-

ing peregrine nesting season.) Other success stories have been the reintro-
duction of the wild turkey and the Atlantic puffin.

Persistence Pays Off

A common sight (and source of dinner) during colonial days, the
wild turkey, North America's largest upland game bird, disappeared from
Maine in the early 1800s, largely due to hunting and loss of woodlands.
Sportsmen tried reintroducing the birds in 1942, but to no avail. In 1977
and 1978, the Maine Department of Inland Fisheries and Wildlife obtained
forty-one wild turkeys from Vermont and released them in the towns of
York and Eliot. In spring of 1982, thirty-three turkeys were trapped from
the growing York County population and released in Waldo County. Two
years later, more birds were relocated, this time to Hancock County, but
poaching was believed to be their downfall. During the winters of 1987
and 1988, seventy wild turkeys were obtained from Connecticut to aug-
ment Maine's growing population. While some have succumbed to heavy
snowfalls, the rest have prospered and multiplied. Today the state's flock
has grown to more than eight thousand and spread well beyond its historic
range. So large is the wild turkey population now that hunting the elusive
birds is once again allowed.

Puffin Patrol

Maine is famous for a multicolored sea bird, the common or Atlantic
puffin. This bird spends most of its time in the North Atlantic, coming
ashore only to breed and raise one chick in an underground burrow. A
century ago, puffins were found on six Maine islands, but excessive hunting led to their near demise in Maine. By the 1900s, there was only one
pair of puffins left south of the Canadian border. The lone couple lived on
Matinicus Rock, a lonely spot twenty-two miles off the coast in Penobscot
Bay. After Matinicus Rock's lighthouse keepers began protecting the puffins from hunters, their numbers began to increase. Today there are about
150 nesting pairs on the rock.

In 1973, Stephen Kress, PhD, a summer resident of Bremen, began
Project Puffin to re-introduce the birds to Eastern Egg Rock in Muscongus Bay. After eight years of trips to Newfoundland to find puffin chicks
to "transplant," his efforts, with help from the National Audubon Society,
paid off. Today, Maine has puffin colonies on at least four of the original
six nesting islands: Eastern Egg Rock, Seal Island, Machias Seal Island, and

Matinicus Rock. Several tour boats operate trips to the puffin colonies from different points along the coast in summer. The puffin-watching season begins around Memorial Day and goes until early to mid-August. For a list of tours, check out mainebirdingtrail.com or visit the Maine Office of Tourism's Web site at visitmaine.com.

Moose Watch

Like puffins and turkeys, moose were once in danger of disappearing in Maine. While explorers in the early 1600s found a plentiful supply of moose throughout New England, unrestricted hunting during the centuries that followed decimated the population. By the early 1900s, only two thousand or so moose were left. Hunting the massive mammals was illegal from 1936 until 1980, and during those years, the animal's numbers slowly grew. In 1979, the moose population had grown so large that a bill allowing the state to issue up to seven hundred hunting permits to Maine resident hunters was signed into law.

Since that time, the number of permits issued and the area open to moose hunting has increased. Nonresidents are also allowed a percentage of the permits. In 1999, three thousand permits were issued, with five hundred of those earmarked specifically for "antlerless moose." In 2013, hunters killed 2,971 moose out of a possible 4,110 permits issued.

In the second edition of *Moving to Maine*, I said that the Department of Inland Fisheries and Wildlife estimated that there are approximately thirty thousand moose in Maine. Today state wildlife biologists put that number between sixty and seventy thousand! That's quite a comeback for an animal that was once nearly eliminated from the state.

More than You Ever Thought You'd Know about Maine Moose

- The Latin name for moose, Alces, means "elk," and in Europe moose are called elk. The animals are the largest members of the deer family.
- Of the four species of moose found in North America, it's the Eastern Moose that calls Maine home.
- Adult cows (females) weigh around eight hundred pounds. Bulls can weigh more than a thousand pounds.
- The total length of a moose is about nine feet. Height measured at the shoulder is about six feet.

🌲 Both cows and bulls have "bells," or skin flaps on the underside of the neck. A cow's bell looks more like a tuft of hair, whereas a bull's bell is larger and rounder.

🌲 The spread of a bull's antlers rarely exceeds sixty-five inches.

🌲 Antlers on cows are extremely rare.

🌲 Moose chomp away on "browse," the leaves and twigs of woody plants. Willow, aspen, birch, maple, pin cherry, and mountain ash are their favorites.

🌲 Moose have no top front teeth.

🌲 They can see only about twenty-five feet.

🌲 Balsam fir is a moose's winter junk food: tasty, but nutritionally lacking.

🌲 Aquatic plants, such as pondweed and water lily, are an important part of a moose's diet.

🌲 Moose begin breeding in late September.

🌲 Cows may produce their first calf when they are two. Each May, cows give birth to one or two calves.

🌲 Calves remain with their mother for one year and are driven off shortly before the next calf is born.

🌲 Black bears, which are common in Maine, are potential predators of moose calves.

🌲 The average life expectancy is eight years for a cow and seven years for a bull. Moose may live into their late teens, but rarely live past twenty.

🌲 Moose are found statewide, but most happily thrive in northern Maine. In the state's Moosehead Lake Region, moose outnumber people three to one.

Deer

According to wildlife biologist Gerry Lavigne, Maine is home to one of the largest subspecies of white-tailed deer, with some mature males, or bucks, weighing nearly four hundred pounds. While more than two hundred thousand of these herbivores call Maine home, it's surprising to note that more deer per square mile (fifteen to twenty-five) live in central and southern sections than in the north, where only two to five deer per square mile can be found. In some particularly popular locales to the south, the Department of Inland Fisheries and Wildlife says there are populations of forty to one hundred deer per square mile.

Increasing numbers of deer (and moose, and even turkeys) mean automobile drivers must exercise caution on Maine roads, particularly at dawn and dusk. Take warning signs seriously—in deer or moose zones drive no faster than the speed limit, use your bright lights, and wear your seat belt. Deer tend to travel in groups, so if you spot one, chances are that others are waiting in the woods. And if a deer or moose is standing in the middle of the road, your best course of action is to slow down, pull over, and exercise patience—honking won't always send them away.

HUNTING SEASON

Avid sportsmen in Maine are in good company—the state has a strong tradition of hunting, fishing, and trapping. Generations of Maine families have hunted in the same quiet spots year after year, or tromped through the spring mud (despite the black flies) to wet a line and fish. Out-of-state hunters and fishermen have headed into the vast woods Down East for more than a century now, staying in remote lodges and employing local guides. Many return to the state each year in search of trophy deer, trout, ducks, or moose.

Fluorescent orange hats, gun racks on pickups, and general stores transformed into tagging stations—all are part of the local scene come fall. Many a new resident has been astonished to meet a camouflaged man with a rifle walking along a woods road, or see a dead deer in a pickup truck on an autumn afternoon. Whether or not you agree with the practice, hunting is a way of life in Maine. And yes, at times the crack of gunfire echoes through the woods.

Although November is the time of year most associated with hunting, seasons for various animals extend into other times of year as well. Deer season, for example, opens for archers in late September and continues through October. Deer hunting with firearms begins in November and lasts until early December. Hunting is not allowed anywhere in the state on Sunday, but it is always advisable to use caution and wear fluorescent orange outerwear when walking in the woods during hunting season.

For more information on hunting regulations, contact your local town office or city hall, or see the Maine Department of Inland Fisheries and Wildlife's Web site at maine.gov/ifw.

Safe Hunting and Land Access

Maine works hard to minimize problems during hunting season. Mike Sawyer, safety officer for the Department of Inland Fisheries and Wildlife, says the state is seeing a definite decrease in hunting accidents, due mainly to safety measures now practiced by many hunters as well as stricter laws and better enforcement. Hunters licensed here must complete an education course, and must wear at least two articles of blaze-orange clothing while hunting. There is also the state's "ID law," which requires hunters to positively identify their target before pulling the trigger.

Respect for property is also an important focus. Maine has a long tradition of allowing reasonable access to unposted land. Given that approximately 94 percent of the land in Maine is privately owned, Maine's Inland Fisheries and Wildlife Landowner Relations Program urges hunters to respect landowners' rights to help ensure that access to and use of private property will continue in years to come. Landowners who do not wish hunting on their property may put up signs accordingly, and may orally or in writing tell others to stay off their property. Rules for posting land may be found at MDIFW's Web site at maine.gov/ifw.

Hunting Licenses

Hunting licenses are available for deer, bear, moose, rabbits, bobcats, and foxes as well as a variety of ducks and fowl. To obtain a hunting license for firearms or archery, present a previous year's license (from Maine or another state) to your local town office, or participating retail store. If you have never hunted, you must present a firearms safety course certificate to the local town office. The certificate is issued after the successful completion of a class on safe hunting given locally once or twice yearly. Archers must also pass a safety course before bow hunting.

You may also meet the requirements to purchase a hunting license online through the Department of Inland Fisheries and Wildlife at: maine.gov/ifw; under "Licenses and Registrations," go to MOSES (Maine Online Sportsman Electronic System).

FISHING

Given the abundance and accessibility of Maine's inland and coastal waterways, the relative simplicity of the gear involved, and the relaxing nature of the sport, it's no wonder fishing is a popular pastime. The images are many: picture a patient fisherman in his ice-fishing shack watching for a "tip-up"; a wader-clad soul fly-casting in a rushing river in late spring; or a group of children jigging for mackerel on a wharf. It's a group of avid anglers around the table at a remote fishing camp, discussing the day's catch while dealing the next poker hand. It's fishing derbies, bait shops, sport-fishing charters, and hatcheries in which millions of trout, slake, and landlocked salmon are raised to stock ponds, lakes, and rivers.

Freshwater Fishing

Last year, anglers caught a variety of freshwater species: brook, lake, and brown trout; smallmouth and largemouth bass; white perch; chain pickerel; and landlocked salmon. Licenses are required for people sixteen and older. Most town offices as well as sporting-goods stores issue licenses, or they can be ordered online from the Inland Fisheries and Wildlife Web site at: maine.gov/ifw; under "Licenses and Registrations," go to MOSES (Maine Online Sportsman Electronic System) or by mail from: Inland Fisheries and Wildlife, 284 State Street, 41 State House Station, Augusta, ME 04333-0041.

It's sad that Maine lakes, ponds, and rivers have not been spared from pollution by mercury. The mercury mostly blows in from out of state and settles into the waters, building up in the bodies of fish. According to the Inland Fisheries and Wildlife Department, fish that eat other fish show the highest mercury levels, and older fish have more mercury than young fish.

To prevent possible harm from consuming mercury, the Maine Bureau of Health offers the following advice: Pregnant and nursing mothers, women who may get pregnant, and children under eight years of age are advised to limit their intake of fish caught in all Maine inland waters to one meal per month. All other individuals are advised to limit their consumption to one meal per week.

Another health concern relates to water birds rather than humans. "Without a doubt, lead poisoning from lead sinkers and jig heads is the number one killer of adult common loons," says Dr. Mark Pokras, assistant professor of wildlife medicine at Tufts University School of Veterinary Medicine. Loons, swans, cranes, and other water birds can die a slow and painful death from lead poisoning after swallowing lead fishing sinkers and jigs lost by anglers.

Fish-eating birds can also ingest the lead if a sinker or jig is still attached to the line or to an escaped fish. For the continued health of these birds, don't use equipment that contains lead.

Saltwater Fishing

The Department of Marine Resources regulates fishing in coastal waters, where anglers hook a variety of ocean dwellers, including pollack, shad, bluefish, Atlantic cod, haddock, redfish, winter flounder, mackerel, bluefin tuna, and striped bass. While saltwater angling licenses are not required for recreational fishing, it's important to note the strict regulations concerning Atlantic salmon and sturgeon. Basically, it is against the law to "angle, take, or possess" these fish from all Maine waters (including coastal waters). Any Atlantic salmon or sturgeon incidentally caught must be released immediately, alive and uninjured, and at no time should the fish be removed from the water.

Special rules also govern fishing for bluefin tuna and striped bass. For current information on size limitations, red tide contamination of shellfish, and other saltwater topics, see the Recreational Marine Fisheries Program's Web site at maine.gov/dmr. As in other parts of the country, many fishermen today free their fish in an effort to promote healthy stocks.

Harvesting Shellfish

Wondering whether you can dig your own clams or pick a bushel of mussels for dinner? Although the state allows anyone to dig up to a half bushel of clams without a license, most coastal communities have ordinances requiring some type of permit, so check with your town office before planning your clambake. Lobsters require a recreational license from the state, which allows use of up to five traps. Snails, whelks, and scallops all require a license as well. (See the Department of Marine Resources (DMR) Web site for particulars: maine.gov/dmr, or call them at 207-633-9500.)

Anyone can pick up to two bushels of mussels without a mussel license; however, when harvesting any seafood, it's wise to check and make sure an area isn't closed due to pollution or red tide. The DMR's shellfish sanitation hotline is constantly updated and can be reached at 800-232-4733.

WILDLIFE HEALTH ISSUES

Rabies

Most people find wildlife watching a rewarding experience. The thrill of spotting a deer, seeing a red-tailed hawk in flight, or glimpsing a porcupine as it shuffles off into the underbrush never seems to diminish. While observing wild animals from a distance is perfectly fine, feeding or petting them is never wise, particularly because of the threat of rabies, a dangerous and lethal disease.

Rabies is a virus that can infect any mammal. The state averages about sixty-five cases of rabies each year, but that number can be higher depending on how mild a winter we have. The southern counties typically have the highest share, although the disease is slowly creeping northward. The Maine Department of Inland Fisheries and Wildlife says that some animals—raccoons, skunks, woodchucks, and foxes—are particularly susceptible to the disease. The department notes that bats are also high-risk carriers, but rodents such as squirrels, rats, mice, and chipmunks very rarely have the disease. (In fact, you should always use extreme caution with bats, alive or dead.)

Thanks to vaccines, rabies is extremely rare among pets and farm animals. How can you tell if a wild animal is rabid? Diseased animals usually behave abnormally, but experts say signs can vary. Some rabid animals appear shy and fearful, while others become aggressive. Still others may simply stumble as though drunk or appear lame. If you believe an animal may be rabid, contact your town's animal control officer. Suspected animals who have come in contact with either a human or domestic animal are tested by the Health and Environmental Testing Laboratory in Augusta.

Maine's Famous Flies

Some Mainers jokingly refer to black flies as the "state bird." The pesky insects are one of four particularly annoying pests in Maine, the other three being mosquitoes, large biting flies (deer, horse, and moose flies), and no-see-ums, or midges. Of these, the black fly probably wins the award for most irritating.

As anyone who has attempted a stroll through the woods in late May knows, black flies are at their hungriest in the spring. Their season lasts roughly from mid-May until the end of June, or as people like to say, "from Mother's Day to Father's Day." The bite of the black fly is tiny, but vicious, causing open wounds and, in some people, noticeable swelling. Mainers cope with the arrival of black flies in sensible ways, wearing light-colored clothing, long sleeves, and a little repellent. Breezes help, too, and early morning is often the best time to be outdoors during black fly season. But take heart: anecdotal evidence suggests that newcomers to black fly territory react most severely to the bites. After a couple of years many people find that their bodies do seem to adjust, and the bites are not so painful and itchy.

Mosquitoes and the larger biting flies can be kept at bay through the use of repellents. Not so for the tiny midges known as no-see-ums. They are most active at dusk and are unfazed by clothing color or most repellents. Their bite is like a tiny pinprick, irritating but not as severe as a black fly's. One annoying characteristic of this tiny creature: its small size means it can sneak through window screens.

Ticks

Two kinds of ticks create headaches for Mainers: wood ticks and deer ticks. The University of Maine Cooperative Extension has a fact sheet with illustrations to help differentiate between the two species on their Web site at extension.umaine.edu. (Click on Insect Pests, Ticks Powassans, Plant Disease, then Insect Fact Sheets.)

The tiny deer tick is a problem because it's capable of transmitting a rare virus called Powassan, as well as Lyme disease, a serious condition causing flu-like symptoms and, in severe cases, arthritis and damage to the nervous system and heart. Two factors to keep in mind are that not all deer ticks carry the bacterium capable of spreading the disease, and, a tick must remain attached to its host for at least twenty-four hours in order to cause infection. Nevertheless, Dr. Sheila Pinette, director of the Maine Center for Disease Control, says that Maine is at the center of a Lyme disease epidemic that stretches south to Delaware and west to Michigan. In 2013, more than 1,375 cases of the disease were reported in Maine.

Experts say that cases of Lyme disease have been reported in every county here and in every season, even during winter when deer stir up ticks that are sheltering in leaf litter.

A new vaccine is in the works but will likely not be ready until 2019. Until that time, experts urge precaution, pesticides, and short lawns. A good Web site with plenty of ideas to help prevent Lyme disease is tick-encounter.org.

Wood ticks have a whitish shield on their backs. This tick readily attaches to humans (as well as our four-legged friends) and is common, particularly in southern Maine. Wood ticks are more annoying than dangerous, although some wood ticks outside of Maine can be the cause of Rocky Mountain spotted fever, a serious disease that can be transmitted to humans. The symptoms of this malady are headache, fever, and aching muscles two to fourteen days after a tick bite.

The brown dog tick is rarely found in Maine—thank goodness! When this type of tick is encountered here, it has hitchhiked from areas south of Massachusetts, most probably on pets and occasionally on clothes.

To prevent bites from ticks, wear hats, pants, and long-sleeved clothing when walking or hiking in the woods and fields. Use repellent and check yourself and your children or pets when you head in from the outdoors. If a deer tick bites you, check with your doctor for signs of Lyme disease, which is treatable, especially when caught early.

7

VACATIONLAND

"I don't have time to have friends come and stay, except on weekends in Maine. I invite a lot of people to come to Maine."

—Martha Stewart, entrepreneur, resident of Deer Isle

When did Maine become "Vacationland?" The state's tourism industry began in earnest in the period following the Civil War, when "sports" from the Northeast were lured to the North Woods by tales of game and adventure, and wealthy families came for the cool coastal breezes. Railroad tracks for Maine Central crisscrossed the state, and steamships from Boston and ports south docked several times daily at coastal wharves. It wasn't long before impressive Victorian resorts began to spring up along the coast, as well as inland on large lakes like Moosehead and Sebago. Soon business was booming. Restaurants served lobster thermidor, yacht clubs held regattas, and dancing pavilions hosted orchestras that played to throngs of summer visitors.

From the beginning, Maine was a haven both for the moneyed and the masses. Summer colonies like those in Bar Harbor, Islesboro, and York Harbor attracted presidents, socialites, and the scions of America's wealthiest families, while nearby honky-tonk beach towns were frequented by working-class families who frolicked in the chilly surf. Religious groups held summer-long revivals here, the tang of the sea air lending a salty counterpoint to the sermons. For tourists then, as now, Maine represented clean air, relaxation, recreation, and nature.

TOURISM TODAY

Not all of the state is a tourist mecca, but chances are, even the sleepiest of towns benefit from the state's popularity in some shape or form. Tax revenues, for instance. In recent years, more than $300 million was brought in to Maine's General Fund to support education, social, and natural resource programs, largely through taxes paid by tourists. Tourism is generally seen as a clean, nonpolluting industry that helps keep historical and cultural sites vibrant and alive, contributes to the protection and preservation of the state's natural resources, and creates cultural and recreational opportunities for Maine residents. Tourism creates economic opportunities as well, enabling many residents the independence of owning their own businesses.

What is it like to live in a vacation paradise? By far, the best benefit is the ability to enjoy year-round what others try to squeeze in during a brief few days. Fishing, hiking, sailing, skiing—the list is practically endless. Living in Maine means taking full advantage of the nearly limitless possibilities this great state provides.

HIKING

The undulating landscape provides hikers with some of the best trekking terrain in the country, from relatively easy jaunts through nature preserves to more challenging climbs up steep mountains where unparalleled vistas await. "There's so much to explore in this state," say Michelle and Bill Davis, who moved here from Atlanta. "The beauty of Maine stretches from one corner to another with vast, pristine, and often undisturbed wilderness and natural areas. It's wonderful to know we now have a lifetime here as residents to leisurely discover the environmental treasures."

Great hikes can be found in every corner in Maine—out almost everyone's back door. In addition, there are four world-class trail systems:

- **Acadia National Park**. Trails and carriage roads in Maine's only national park take day hikers up over coastal mountains, offering remarkable prospects of sea and shore (nps.gov/acad/index.htm).
- **Appalachian Trail**. The famous hiking highway runs 276 miles through Maine, from the New Hampshire border to the Appalachian Trail's northern terminus at Mount Katahdin. Many who have hiked the whole trail call Maine's section the most beautiful. For information, see nps.gov.

🌲 **Baxter State Park**. Home of Mount Katahdin, the "forever wild" backcountry park has more than fifty interconnecting trails that ramble for hundreds of miles, across peaks and to remote ponds. Some of the most beautiful scenery in Maine can be found within the bounds of the park. Reservations (required for overnight stays) are limited and in great demand. See baxterstateparkauthority.com.

🌲 **White Mountain National Forest**. Many are surprised to learn that close to fifty thousand acres of this national forest, normally associated with New Hampshire, are located along Maine's western border, allowing access to more than two hundred interconnecting trails (fs.usda.gov/whitemountain).

For information on hikes in your area, contact your local chamber of commerce, the indispensable DeLorme *Maine Atlas and Gazetteer*, the Appalachian Mountain Club's excellent *Maine Mountain Guide*, or the Maine Outdoor Adventure Club at moac.org, an all-volunteer member organization that celebrated twenty-five years of exploring Maine's outdoors in 2014.

The Ten Highest Peaks in Maine

Name	County	Height Above Sea Level	Relative Climb Above Base
Katahdin	Piscataquis	5,267	4,674
Sugarloaf	Franklin	4,237	2,931
Old Speck	Oxford	4,180	2,690
Crocker	Franklin	4,168	2,949
Bigelow	Somerset	4,150	3,028
No. Brother	Piscataquis	4,143	1,323
Saddleback	Franklin	4,116	2,596
Abraham	Franklin	4,049	2,809
The Horn	Franklin	4,023	2,923
Spaulding	Franklin	3,988	2,748

State Parks

Maine is home to more than thirty state parks, which are enjoyed by residents yearlong. Twelve state parks and the Allagash Wilderness Waterway provide camping, and a number of sites require reservations. For more information about the reservation system, see the Bureau of Parks and Lands Web site at maine.gov/doc/parks. In addition to camping, state parks provide the dramatic backdrop for a range of day-use activities, from picnicking to ocean swimming. Here's a sampling, including some of the lesser-known gems.

🌲 **Aroostook State Park**. Maine's first state park! On Echo Lake south of Presque Isle, this 577-acre park offers hiking on 1,213-foot Quaggy Joe Mountain and trout fishing on Echo Lake, as well as campsites, a bathhouse, and a beach with a lifeguard. Groomed cross-country ski trails are available when the snow flies. 207-768-8341.

🌲 **Damariscotta Lake State Park**. A family favorite in Jefferson, this lakeside park is known for its sand beach, patrolled by lifeguards. It's also a popular place for picnics on summer evenings, with its group shelter and grills. 207-549-7600.

🌲 **Grafton Notch State Park**. Some of Maine's better hiking crisscrosses this mountainous park north of Bethel—several trails extend through the Mahoosuc Range. But you don't have to be a trekker to enjoy the state park here. It also features several stunning roadside gorges. 207-824-2912.

🌲 **Moose Point State Park**. On Route 1 between Belfast and Searsport, Moose Point is one of Maine's smaller and lesser-known state parks. Those in the know enjoy its picnic facilities, short but fun hiking trail, and exceptional views of Penobscot Bay. 207-548-2882.

🌲 **Peaks–Kenney State Park**. Another of the state's less-busy parks, this beauty sits on lovely Sebec Lake just north of the picturesque community of Dover-Foxcroft. There's a swimming beach, camping facilities, and great upcountry vistas. 207-564-2003.

🌲 **Roque Bluffs State Park**. Just south of Jonesboro, this Down East area has one of the few pebble beaches in Maine as well as a freshwater pond. Hardy swimmers take to the waters here and picnickers enjoy the ocean breezes. 207-255-3475.

🌲 **Swan Lake State Park**. North of Swanville, Maine's newest state park provides swimming and a playground. 207-525-4404.

🌲 **Wolfe's Neck Woods State Park**. What makes this park unique is its proximity to bustling downtown Freeport. Only 4.5 miles from L.L. Bean, Wolfe's Neck sits on more than two hundred acres and offers guided trails, picnic tables, and views of Casco Bay and the Harraseeket River. 207-865-4465.

ON THE WATER

Sea Kayaking

With more than 3,500 miles of coast, as many islands, and innumerable bays and coves, Maine is a paddler's paradise. Quite aside from the state's renowned natural beauty, it's also home to the Maine Island Trail, a network of islands along the length of the coast open to conscientious visitors (mita.org).

There are outfitters from Kittery to Calais offering sales, rentals, and guided half-day and full-day trips, including equipment to keep you safe and dry. After a short clinic, you'll be ready to paddle off on a coastal adventure. The Office of Tourism site has loads of sea kayaking information. The site is www.visitmaine.com.

Canoeing

As Maine guides and the natives before them knew, canoes are the perfect vessel for exploring lakes and ponds, allowing paddlers to get right up close and personal to the water. Maine's premier canoe company, Old Town, has an interesting Web site offering information on the heritage of the Maine canoe plus loads of links to other sites—oldtowncanoe.com. One of the state's most popular canoeing destinations is the Allagash River Waterway, a world-famous chain of lakes and rivers stretching for close to one hundred miles in the northern part of Maine. The state has a wealth of canoe outfitters ready to send you paddling downriver or across a tranquil pond. Check out visitmaine.com for more ideas.

Paddleboarding

"SUP" or stand-up paddleboarding has really caught on in Maine's lakes and coves, and is fast becoming one of our most popular water sports. Devotees say paddleboarding is great exercise and an easy way to explore scenic waterways. Although harder to find to rent than either kayaks or canoes, a growing number of outfitters are providing lessons and opportunities for this Zen-like experience. L.L. Bean offers discovery and introductory lessons starting at just $20 at a variety of locations—including at the flagship store in Freeport.

Ten Largest Lakes in Maine

Maine is dotted with more than twenty-five hundred lakes and ponds. Not all allow boats or personal watercraft, so check first with local authorities or the area chamber of commerce. Here are Maine's very biggest bodies of fresh water:

Name	Town	Square Miles
Moosehead	Little Squaw Township	117.02
Sebago	Sebago	44.95
Chesuncook	T3 R12 WELS	36.05
Flagstaff	Flagstaff Township	31.72
Pemadumcook	T1 R10 WELS	28.59
Spednic	Vanceboro	26.90
Mooselookmeguntic	Richardson Township	25.47
Grand Lake (east)	Forest City Township	25.11
Grand Lake (west)	T5 ND BPP	22.41
Chamberlain	T7 R12 WELS	17.32

Whitewater Rafting

Northern Maine offers exciting class III to class V whitewater from early May to early October on the Kennebec, Penobscot, and Dead rivers. Because of controlled dam releases from hydroelectric plants, Maine is the only state in the Northeast that can guarantee high water, along with unmatched scenery and wildlife. Two rivers, the Kennebec and the Dead, converge at The Forks, headquarters for most of Maine's rafting companies. The West Branch of the Penobscot, largest of the three rivers, flows a few miles from towering Mt. Katahdin. For more information, call Raft Maine at 207-824-3694 or see their Web site at raftmaine.com.

Sailing

Some yachters have claimed that island-studded Penobscot Bay offers the best sailing this side of the Mediterranean. And that's only the start. For literally hundreds of years, the state's 3,700 miles of seacoast have been considered a sailor's dream. Deep harbors, quiet coves, good anchorages, and thousands of islands add up to memorable cruising trips, whether your vessel is a twenty-eight-foot sloop or fifty-foot yacht. If you don't (yet) own a boat, take a two-hour day sail on an historic vessel or spend several days aboard a Maine Windjammer. You'll quickly see why many believe Maine offers the very best sailing in the world (mainewindjammercruises.com).

And what if you'd like to learn? Many coastal and lake-rich communities offer ways for residents and visitors to pick up this ancient skill. From yacht clubs to town-owned programs, children and adults alike can practice trimming sails, tying knots, and yelling "Boom coming over!"

One such program is Rockland's Apprenticeshop, a school for traditional boatbuilding and seamanship, offering adult sailing lessons through Rockland Community Sailing. The "hands-on" approach teaches rigging and de-rigging, the winds and points of sail, leaving and landing on the dock, steering, tacking, and jibing, sail trim, basic chart reading, and safety. Instructors customize the course to cover additional topics such as anchoring, basic navigation, moorings, reefing, heavy weather tactics, and more (apprenticeshop.org).

IN THE SNOW

Cross-Country Skiing

No matter where you live in Maine, once the snowflakes fall you're not far from a place to cross-country ski. This winter sport has been part of Maine's heritage since 1870. Some say it was even introduced to the United States here, when the Swedish immigrants who founded the Aroostook County village of New Sweden brought with them their traditional ten-foot wooden skis with leather bindings. Today's Nordic skiers have more sophisticated equipment, but they enjoy the same beautiful countryside as did those early enthusiasts.

The state has several fancy cross-country ski centers with groomed trails, and there are miles of virtually unlimited backcountry skiing through Maine's woods and fields, across golf courses, and in parks. Favorite sites are Acadia National Park in Bar Harbor and the Bethel Nordic Ski Center. See the Ski Maine Association (skimaine.com) for more information.

Snowmobiling

Thousands of miles of signed, groomed snowmobile trails interconnect across Maine like mini-highways, circling frozen lakes, winding through snowcapped spruces, and meandering along country roads. Festivals, poker runs, organized rides, hill climbs, and radar runs keep scores of sledders and snowmobile clubs busy throughout the colder months. For more information on trails, you can visit the Maine Snowmobiling Association at mesnow.com.

Alpine Skiing and Snowboarding

"Maine is blessed with a wide variety of ski areas," says Greg Sweetser, executive director of the Ski Maine Association. "We've got everything from world-class resorts like Sunday River and Sugarloaf to classic community areas like the Camden Snow Bowl, where you can see the ocean from the top of Ragged Mountain. There are underdeveloped big mountains with unmatched scenery, like Saddleback and Big Squaw, and everything in between."

If you enjoy downhill skiing or snowboarding, a clear advantage to living in the state is proximity to the slopes. From Lonesome Pine Trails in Fort Kent to Shawnee Peak in Bridgton (northern New England's largest night-skiing mountain) most Mainers live within an easy drive of short lift lines, superior snow, and uncrowded trails. And unlike slopes in the west, several of Maine's ski areas are alongside beautiful lakes, making for more activities available year-round. "There are a variety of programs for all ages, too," adds Greg Sweetser. "Race leagues, learn-to-ski or -board clinics, women's programs—you name it."

Youngsters in Maine have the opportunity to learn downhill sports at an early age. "Many communities have really strong programs in place where kids four to twelve learn how to ski," notes Sweetser. "Even Portland and Bangor, which you wouldn't think of as ski towns, have school programs." The Maine Ski Association also sponsors the Fifth Grade Ski Pass, in which every fifth-grader in the state can enjoy free skiing and snowboarding at many Maine mountains.

For a complete list of ski areas, check the Maine Ski Association's Web site at skimaine.com.

OUTDOOR EDUCATION

Whether you want to learn to tie your own flies or master the J-stroke, a course at one of Maine's outdoor-education schools can show you the ropes. Take up a new sport, perfect one you already enjoy, or become a knowledgeable registered Maine guide. Outdoor courses are a great way to get to know Maine and Mainers fast.

🌲 **Kittery Trading Post**, Kittery. Maine's second-most-famous outfitter offers instruction in kayaking, fly-fishing, fly-tying, and hunting (kitterytradingpost.com).

🌲 **L.L. Bean Outdoor Discovery Program**, Freeport. The sporting goods giant provides a wealth of resources and instruction year-round in everything from wingshooting to bicycling to moose photography (llbean.com/outdoors).

🌲 **Maine Sport Outdoor School**, Rockport. Known for its kayaking courses and trips, Maine Sport also offers courses in becoming a registered Maine guide and wilderness medicine (mainesport.com).

🌲 **Maine Bound**, Orono. An amazing resource based at the University of Maine, Maine Bound grew from an outing club to an outfitter to a provider of instruction. Rent everything from canoes to crampons at reasonable prices, sign up for a mountaineering course, or head out on an ice-climbing expedition. Call 207-581-1794 for more information, or see umaine.edu/mainebound.

🌲 **Maine Audubon Society**, Falmouth. From its nature centers in Falmouth and Holden (outside of Bangor), Maine Audubon offers a host of field trips and classes in subjects from bird watching to plant identification. Very reasonably priced, these seminars will help you quickly get to know your way around your Maine backyard (maineaudubon.org).

🌲 **The Nature Conservancy**, Brunswick. Workshops and outings have become a regular offering of this well-known conservation organization. See rare species up close or canoe a newly saved river. See nature.org and click on Maine.

LIGHTHOUSES

Maine is justifiably famous for its lighthouses, with the American Lighthouse Foundation headquartered in Rockland. Here's a partial list, beginning in York and proceeding Down East along the coast. Included are only those beacons where close-up views are possible. For a complete list, see lighthousefriends.com.

🌲 **Cape Neddick**, York. A forty-one-foot white cast-iron conical tower, on the summit of Cape Neddick Nubble, this coastal sentinel was built in 1879.

🕯 **Spring Point Ledge**, South Portland. A white brick and cast-iron cylindrical tower, the light at Spring Point illuminates the west side of the main channel of Portland Harbor. It was built in 1897.

🕯 **Portland Head Light**, Cape Elizabeth. Maine's most famous and most recognizable light, this eighty-foot white fieldstone and brick tower was built in 1791 under the authorization of George Washington.

🕯 **Pemaquid Light**, Pemaquid Point. The Pemaquid peninsula's thirty-two-foot, conical fieldstone tower was built in 1827 and is a popular place to watch crashing surf.

🕯 **Monhegan Light**, Monhegan Island. Atop the enchanting mid-coast island, the Monhegan Light was constructed in 1824 and looks out across Monhegan Harbor and nearby Manana Island.

🕯 **Marshall Point Light**, Port Clyde (St. George). A twenty-five-foot white granite tower with an oft-photographed footbridge, Marshall Point Light was erected in 1832.

🕯 **Rockland Breakwater Light**, Rockland. While it's a small light-house by Maine standards, the eighteen-foot square tower atop the Rockland Breakwater's fog signal house is among the most fun to visit because it sits at the end of a mile-long stone breakwater that juts clear into the middle of the harbor.

🕯 **Owls Head Light**, Owls Head. Built in 1825, this is a twenty-foot white conical tower, constructed of brick.

🕯 **Grindel Point Light**, Islesboro. Accessible by car ferry from Lin-colnville, this tall island sentinel was built in 1851.

🕯 **Bass Harbor Head Light**, Bass Harbor. Built in 1858, this twenty-six-foot cylindrical tower sits on a ledge on Mount Desert Island's "quiet side," and attracts some spillover tourist traffic from Acadia National Park.

🕯 **West Quoddy Head Light**, Lubec. Set dramatically above soar-ing cliffs at the easternmost Maine point and looking out at the Bay of Fundy, this forty-nine-foot tower is the state's only red-and-white painted light. Great hiking trails wander along the shore and through the woods of the surrounding state park.

COVERED BRIDGES

Once there were 120 covered bridges in the state of Maine, but most were lost to fire, flood, ice, and "progress." Here's a list of nine covered bridges, and the rivers they cross, from the Maine Office of Tourism. If you'd like more information, consult the Maine Department of Transportation's Web site at maine.gov/mdot/historicbridges/coveredbridges.

- **Babb's Bridge**. Crossing the Presumpscot River, Babb's is Maine's oldest covered bridge, built in 1843. It is located off the River Road, between the towns of Gorham and Windham. Burned in 1973, it has since been rebuilt.

- **Hemlock Bridge**. Located off Route 302 in the town of Fryeburg, this old bridge spans a channel of the Saco River. Built in 1857, it is of Paddleford truss construction with supporting laminated wooden arches.

- **Low's Bridge**. Originally built in 1857, carried away when the Piscataquis River flooded in 1987, and rebuilt in 1990, this structure connects the upcountry villages of Sangerville and Guilford.

- **Sunday River Bridge**. Also known as "the Artists' Bridge," this span is the most painted and photographed bridge in the state. It was built in 1872 in Newry.

- **Porter Bridge**. Constructed as a joint project by the towns of Porter and Parsonsfield, Porter Bridge is a unique two-span structure, put in place above the Ossipee River in 1876.

- **Robyville Bridge**. Situated above Kenduskeag Stream, this Corinth span is the only completely shingled covered bridge in Maine.

- **Lovejoy Bridge**. At only seventy feet long, Lovejoy Bridge is the shortest covered bridge in Maine. It's perched above the Ellis River in the town of Andover.

- **Bennet Bridge**. Spanning the Magalloway River in Lincoln Plantation, this relatively young bridge was built in 1901.

- **Watson Settlement Bridge**. In the town of Littleton, the Watson Settlement Bridge has two distinctions: it is the newest covered bridge—built in 1911—and also the farthest north in Maine.

EXPLORING WATERS AND SKY

Maine State Aquarium (maine.gov/dmr/rm/aquarium). Located on the water in West Boothbay Harbor, the aquarium is operated by the Maine Department of Marine Resources and features many interactive exhibits, extraordinary lobsters of all sizes and colors, and even a giant seventeen-pound lobster and his mammoth claws.

Mount Desert Oceanarium (theoceanarium.com). This museum features a harbor seal exhibit, lobster museum, and salt marsh trails.

Bar Harbor Whale Museum (barharborwhalemuseum.org). Maine's gentle giants of the deep are celebrated here.

Emera Astronomy Center at the University of Maine, Orono (astro.umaine.edu). The brand-new home of the Maynard F. Jordan Planetarium and the coolest place to stargaze (other than your backyard!) in Maine. Call 207-581-1341 for information.

GOLF

Mainers love their links, and the state offers close to forty eighteen-hole courses and more than sixty nine-hole courses scattered across the landscape. Many are challenging; virtually all are breathtakingly beautiful. Two are considered premier courses: Rockport's Samoset Golf Club, known as the "Pebble Beach of the East," and the Sugarloaf Golf Club located in Carrabassett Valley. A third course, the Belgrade Lakes Golf Club, was recently rated the fifth-best "New Upscale" course in the country by *Golf Digest* magazine.

Portland is home to the Maine Golf Hall of Fame (mainegolfhalloffame.com), which keeps a roll of honor going all the way back to 1993. For a complete list of courses in Maine, see the Maine Office of Tourism Web site at visitmaine.com.

PROFESSIONAL SPORTS TEAMS

In addition to NCAA champion university and college squads, Maine has three professional sports teams, the Portland Sea Dogs, Maine Red Claws, and Portland Pirates.

"This is a state where you don't have to take out a loan to take your family to a professional baseball, basketball, or hockey game," say Michelle and Bill Davis. "The ticket costs are affordable and the games are fun without the heavy crowds and parking issues found in major cities. It's easy to be reminded that you're in Maine, however, when the contest of the night is 'who has the dirtiest car in the parking garage?'"

♟ **Maine Red Claws** (nba.com/dleague/maine). Affiliated with the Boston Celtics, the Red Claws shoot hoops in the Portland Expo

Building and are part of the NBA Development League. Back in 2009, a contest was held to choose the new team's moniker, with "Red Claws" chosen as the winner. Not only does the name and logo hark back to the state's lobster industry, but the use of "Red" pays tribute to longtime Boston Celtics Coach Red Auerbach.

- **Portland Sea Dogs** (portlandseadogs.com). Established in 1994, the Sea Dogs are the Double-A affiliate of the Boston Red Sox, and a trip to cheer them on at Hadlock Field (complete with the Maine Monster, a thirty-seven-foot-tall replica of Fenway Park's Green Monster) is fun for the whole family. Seats are close enough to see all the action, tickets are cheap, and the players play for the love of the game.

- **Portland Pirates** (portlandpirates.com). Exciting American League Hockey is played at the newly refurbished Cumberland County Civic Center each winter, where the crowd cheers on the swashbuckling Pirates.

PROFILE—THE MOVE THAT WAS MEANT TO BE

Ben and Vicki Corrington arrived in the Pine Tree State from the south in 2005. "My wife is a native," says Ben, so we have visited Maine ever since we met. We were married here, and visited annually, and thought we'd end up here someday." When Vicki's sister became ill in the summer of 2004, she came up from Georgia for weeks at a time to help with her recovery. "It came to a head one day in August," remembers Ben, "when the four of us were having lunch at the Waterfront restaurant on a perfect day. The sky was clear, the schooners were coming and going in the harbor, when I looked over at Vicki and she was crying. Not sad, but at the perfection of it all. I knew then we'd be moving here sooner rather than later, while I had one more practice startup left in me." Ben is a chiropractor, while Vicki is a personal coach. "After we made the decision, and considered what had to occur for it all to happen, everything fell into place freakishly easily at both ends. Makes you think it was meant to be."

8

CULTURAL MAINE

"Unlike much of the rest of New England which has been vastly 'colonized' by urbanites, Maine seems to have retained much more of its 'rough around the edges' character and feels more authentically 'New England' to me."

—Richard Blanco, poet, resident of Bethel

For centuries, Maine has been an inspiration for artists, musicians, and writers—such as Richard Blanco of Bethel, the inaugural poet for Barack Obama's second inauguration—yet one of the biggest fears of new residents is that a move to Maine means exile from the world of intellect and culture. "I questioned whether I could put myself in a rural situation and not miss the culture and hubbub of Boston," says Dottie Paradis of Cornish.

The longing for the bright lights of a big city prompted Dottie to take frequent pilgrimages back to the bustle. "I travel far and wide for cultural stimulation," says Dottie Paradis. "It's a lot of miles, but one trip to Portland will last me about a week. I travel to Boston about once a month."

Cherie Scott of Boothbay sometimes misses the crowded streets of her hometown city in India. The author of the "Mumbai to Maine" blog (mumbaitomaine.com) says "Maine has slowed me down. I've gotten used to it. I hate to admit it, but I have come to enjoy the legato tempo of Maine life. But there are days when my heart pines for the chaos and bustle of the sardine-packed city of Mumbai—my original hometown."

Clearly, a rural or small-town lifestyle does not have all of the cultural perks of urban living; nor, of course, does it have the problems of urban living. But the question remains: Is culture lacking in the Pine Tree State, or is it a question of perception?

"We're happy and pleased that we made the move to Maine," says Carol Doherty-Cox of Port Clyde. "We investigated various areas on the Internet and were impressed with the information we found on the midcoast area in particular. But we've heard stories from others who've had difficulty adjusting to the lack of shopping or their (perceived) cultural isolation."

Most newcomers are pleasantly surprised to discover that Maine has much more to offer than lighthouses and loons. Ruth Anne and Wesley Hohfeld comment, "We are continually pleased with the varied and regular offerings of theater, creative arts, and culture. We'd expected to go to Boston and New York for stimulation." In fact, the state boasts a wealth of cultural and educational activities to keep most people happily enriched—museums of all kinds, theater in all settings, music of all varieties, and scores of festivals, workshops, and classes.

Some new residents find their new, less stressful lifestyles give them leave to participate in or try activities they couldn't find time for before. "I've started studying piano since we moved to Maine," says Lynda Chilton. "With my hectic lifestyle in Virginia, that just wasn't an option."

"For me, the biggest advantage to living in Maine is the small-town feeling with big-city availability," says Barry Hurtt of Cushing. "From wonderful little bookstores, to Maine PBS, to the variety of arts and music—there is actually too much available."

What also surprises new residents is the quality of activities available away from the state's larger cities. "There are excellent concerts and theater programs in Down East Maine," says Marlene Kinlin of Jonesport. "And I've audited courses at the University of Maine in Machias that were terrific."

Only in Maine can you learn to build a Friendship sloop, hear a Bach cantata performed by the country's oldest symphony orchestra, and rub elbows with the founder of a multinational computer company at a cutting-edge technological conference. Maine offers its residents diverse opportunities that aren't usually found in a rural state: the chance to study Russian with a native, for example, or play the harp at a world-renowned harp colony, or take in an exhibit of Andrew Wyeth's paintings in a highly regarded museum not far from where they were painted.

You can tour a Shaker village, visit Revolutionary War General Henry Knox's mansion, or hitch a ride on an antique steam train. Not only that, but you can see just about any world-class performance you'd like at many of the state's auditoriums and theaters. As more than one newcomer has discovered, there's a heck of a lot to do here.

HIGHER EDUCATION

The University of Maine System

One important source of cultural activities reaching all corners of Maine is the University of Maine System (maine.edu). Seven universities—some with multiple campuses—are located across the state, as well as eight University College outreach centers, a law school, an additional thirty-one course sites, Cooperative Extension, and "Online Maine," a combination of online and classroom learning. A common board of trustees and a chancellor oversee the schools, but each university has its own president, faculty, and administration.

The system's flagship school is located in Orono, twelve miles from Bangor, and is called simply the University of Maine, or "UMaine." It is a four-year residential university with five colleges—Business, Public Policy, and Health; Education and Human Development; Engineering; Liberal Arts and Science; and Natural Sciences, Forestry, and Agriculture. It's particularly well known for its forestry and engineering departments, although the past two decades have seen a big expansion of its biotechnological research facilities and programs, which now include numerous research and teaching laboratories.

Residents enjoy many benefits due to the university's presence. World-class performances at the Maine Center for the Arts, three on-campus museums, and Division–I sports teams (including the 1999 NCAA champion men's hockey team) are just a few examples.

The second-largest institution in the University of Maine System, the University of Southern Maine (USM), offers graduate degrees in law, business, computer science, manufacturing management, and many other fields. USM (usm.maine.edu) is a major force in southern Maine's business community, offering special courses, training programs, computer learning centers, technical assistance, and research services. The university is also a cultural power, sponsoring performances of all kinds and offering adult-ed classes and free lectures to the public.

The other University of Maine campuses and outreach centers also contribute much to their surrounding communities: drama, dance, and music performances; art exhibits and museums; sporting events; access to services such as libraries and athletic facilities; and, of course, the opportunity for lifelong learning. Within the state there is excellent public support for the University System, with Maine voters approving bond referendums in the past few elections. As with far too many other states, there are budget deficit problems plaguing Maine, but trustees and others are working to bridge the gap and keep the universities sustainable.

Another institution that is making more and more contributions to the culture of southern Maine is the University of New England, an independent, coeducational school whose charter dates from 1831. The university (une.edu) has three distinct campuses—the main campus, located on a beautiful oceanside site in Biddeford; a Portland campus; and, as of 2014, a new campus in Tangier, Morocco.

The University of New England has graduate and undergraduate degree programs focused on the health and life sciences, human services, management, education, and the liberal arts. It also is home to Maine's only medical school, the University of New England College of Osteopathic Medicine, which emphasizes the education of primary-care physicians. The College of Dental Medicine, opened in the fall of 2013, is the only one of its kind in Northern New England.

Colleges

Maine is also home to many fine colleges. Three—Bates, located in Lewiston; Bowdoin, in the heart of Brunswick; and Colby, overlooking Waterville—are listed among the top twenty-five liberal arts colleges in the nation. Others, such as the College of the Atlantic in Bar Harbor, Husson College in Bangor, Unity College in Unity, and Maine College of Art in Portland, bring inquisitive learners to the state and offer residents a wealth of activities to enjoy. From free lectures on wellness to performances of *Macbeth*, from jazz ensembles to modern dance performances, these small colleges alone have enough cultural and educational activities to keep anyone happily stimulated most of the year. Some—such as Bowdoin College—even allow area seniors to audit courses at no charge.

A new era of higher education began in 2003 with the transition of Maine's technical colleges to the new community college system. Established by Former Governor John Baldacci, the switch is more than just a change in name. Maine's seven community colleges offer more classes than ever, with courses in high-growth areas such as telecommunications, computers, and electronics, as well as traditional trades, along with free, customized pre-employment training for qualified businesses. Since the transition, enrollment at Maine's community colleges has grown 58 percent, to 10,188 students. Maine joins forty-five other states that have community college systems in place to prepare students for the workplace with a two-year course of studies or for four-year degree programs at state and private colleges and universities. For residents of Wells, South Portland, Calais, Auburn, Bangor, Fairfield, and Presque Isle, where the colleges are located, these schools offer opportunities for community enrichment in activities such as continuing education and exhibits.

PROFILE—CAME TO MAINE FOR COLLEGE, AND STAYED

Amy and Scott Bottomley both came to Maine as students at the University of New England (UNE) in Biddeford Pool; Amy, from Vermont, and Scott, from New Hampshire. They were drawn to UNE because of the school's beautiful location, as well as its Division–III athletics. Scott played soccer while at UNE, and Amy ran cross country and was on the swim team.

"We officially became Maine residents in 2011, after graduate school for our Doctor of Physical Therapy degrees," says Amy. "We waited until then because we did not know if we would stay in Maine. When it came time to decide, there was no question. Not only had we lived in Maine for the majority of our lives, but most of our friends were here. We choose to live in Bethel, primarily for the skiing and hiking. We'd started skiing at Sunday River while in college and explored the area from there."

Amy says she thinks Maine and Vermont are very similar in a lot of respects. "Little things are the same, like getting money back on returnable bottles. While that seems silly, we have a lot of friends from other states that have no idea about things like that."

ADULT EDUCATION

An incredible array of courses are available through local high schools and community centers. From stargazing to massage therapy, conversational Italian to Public Speaking 101, Maine residents can brush up on subjects or become immersed in entirely new fields of study—and at a very reasonable cost. Look in the phone book under school districts or search the Web for adult education offerings in your area.

MAINE PUBLIC BROADCASTING

The Maine Public Broadcasting Network (mpbn.org) takes its mission to engage the minds and enrich the lives of Mainers seriously. Available to all Maine people every day, MPBN was previously known as Maine Public Broadcasting Corporation. It was created in 1992 with the merger of Maine's two public broadcasting systems (WCBB, founded by Colby, Bates, and Bowdoin colleges in 1961; and MPBN, founded by the University of Maine System).

The Maine Public Broadcasting Network broadcasts award-winning television (Maine PBS) and radio programming, creates special programs for Maine's schools and businesses, and has an excellent Web site. A statewide vote—passed by nearly 65 percent of those who voted—earmarked funds for the network's transition from analog to digital, and the service was launched statewide on May 21, 2002.

Maine Public Television broadcasts about nineteen hours a day on Channel 10 in central Maine, Channel 26 in southern Maine, Channel 12 in northern Maine, and Channel 13 in eastern Maine. Its broadcast area covers the entire state, even venturing into New Hampshire and New Brunswick, and is available in "podcast" formats. All in all, Maine PBS covers an area of approximately five hundred thousand households.

In addition to carrying the popular PBS programs such as *Nova* and *Masterpiece Theatre*, Maine Public Television produces a substantial amount of original programming on local people and local issues. Among the local productions Mainers tune in to are: *Made in Maine, MaineWatch, True North*, and *Capitol Connection.*

One surprise for newcomers who tune into Maine Public Television occurs in February, during the high school basketball playoffs, when the network airs both the boys' and girls' championship games. "It's the only place I have ever been where *The NewsHour* is preempted by local high school basketball," says Carole Brand. The explanation for this annual disruption may lie in something former Celtics point guard Bob Cousy once mused: "Indiana gets credit for having the most rabid basketball fans in the union, but Maine is a very, very active basketball state."

Maine Public Radio hit the airwaves in 1970. It broadcasts on seven FM stations throughout the state: WMED Calais 89.7; WMEA Portland 90.1; WMEP Camden 90.5; WMEH Bangor 90.9; WMEW Waterville 91.3; WMEM Presque Isle 106.1; and WMEF Fort Kent 106.5.

More than 120,000 listeners each week enjoy comprehensive local news coverage, classical music, and programming from National Public Radio and Public Radio International. Many Mainers are devoted listeners, and MPBN is a frequent winner of broadcasting awards.

LIBRARIES

Maine's libraries are precious pearls scattered throughout the state. Many are housed in historic buildings that speak volumes about the state's history with their presence alone. All are linked through technology in a high-tech Internet necklace of information that makes researching and learning a snap. Maine's librarians just may be the most knowledgeable in the country, or perhaps it is their willingness to be helpful and pleasant that makes consulting them such a productive joy.

In addition to books, Maine's libraries big and small provide online assistance and access to periodicals, including magazines and newspapers, and they sponsor a host of public meetings and activities.

For a comprehensive list of the state's public, school, academic, state agency, and special libraries, check out mainelibraries.com. Many local libraries have their own Web pages, so you can see what's going on in specific institutions around the state.

CULTURAL ACTIVITIES

Below is a sampling of cultural offerings available throughout the state. While this list is by no means complete, it gives a good idea of the variety of opportunities available at all times of the year. Phone numbers or Web sites are provided so you can check on particulars.

Theater

Since the days of nineteenth-century summer theater, Mainers have enjoyed all kinds of theatrical performances, from Shakespeare under the stars to old-time vaudeville to modern one-acts. There are professional companies, festivals with touring productions, and civic theaters where the local chief of police may have the starring role. Venues include historic old opera houses, converted churches and train stations, as well as more conventional auditoriums and theaters. Here's a sampling of what you might find:

- ⚑ **The Belfast Maskers Theatre**. This group performs in a converted station house on the old Belfast/Moosehead railroad along the Belfast waterfront. Luminaries who have appeared with the Maskers over their twelve-year history include Liv Ullmann and Ali MaCgraw (belfastmaskers.com).
- ⚑ **Camden Civic Theatre**. This talented ensemble of local actors performs year-round in the restored Camden Opera House, an elegant setting for entertainment of all types in the heart of downtown. Recent productions included *Oliver!* and *Music Man* (camdencivictheater.com).
- ⚑ **The Lincoln Theater**. Lincoln Theater's mission is to be a "major community resource for the promotion and production of the performing arts." Hosting plays, movies, concerts, and even town meetings, the historic building in Damariscotta is doing just that (lcct.org).
- ⚑ **Deertrees Theatre and Cultural Center**. Nestled in the woods of western Maine, Deertrees is listed on both Maine's Register of Historic Landmarks and the National Register of Historic Places. The building was the dream of an opera coach from the New York Metropolitan Opera Company and was constructed in 1933 in Harrison, on the site of a former deer run. It was restored in 1984 through the efforts of a community group and hosts a variety of theatrical performances (deertrees-theatre.org).
- ⚑ **Figures of Speech Theatre**. Figures of Speech is a twenty-four-year-old, nationally known touring company in Freeport whose actors are accompanied by live music and a cast of imaginative puppets (figures.org).
- ⚑ **Lakewood Theatre**. The theater company at Lakewood has been performing for a century on tranquil Lake Wesserunsett in Skowhegan, in a glen surrounded by a grove of towering birches. Productions include seven regular-season plays, plus reprises, children's shows, and a theater camp for kids age six to sixteen years old (lakewoodtheater.org).
- ⚑ **Mad Horse Theatre**. One of the state's premier drama troupes, Mad Horse in Portland often performs in collaboration with local playwrights and USM students (madhorse.com).

🌲 **Maine State Music Theatre**. Maine's only professional music theater has been playing to sell-out crowds in Brunswick for more than forty years. The group performs favorite musicals in the newly renovated Pickard Theater on the campus of Bowdoin College (msmt.org).

🌲 **Ogunquit Playhouse**. "America's Foremost Summer Theatre" offers ten weeks of productions in a 750-seat restored, converted barn. Since opening in 1933, the cast of performers in the outstanding productions at the playhouse has included Lee Remick, Basil Rathbone, Art Carney, Sally Struthers, and scores of others (ogunquitplayhouse.org).

🌲 **Penobscot Theatre Company**. In 1997, the Penobscot Theatre acquired the historic Bangor Opera House, a beautiful locale built in 1888. Performances are held there, as well as outside on the banks of the Penobscot River during the warmer months (penobscottheatre.org).

🌲 **The Theater At Monmouth**. Designated by the state legislature in 1975 as "The Shakespearean Theatre of Maine," this company presents the work of the old bard in the century-old Cumston's Hall. It's an intimate setting (275 seats) in which plays are performed in rotating repertory (theateratmonmouth.org).

Art

Over the last century, Maine has become synonymous with fine art, having inspired generations of internationally recognized artists such as Rockwell Kent, Winslow Homer, Marsden Hartley, Louise Nevelson, and the Wyeth family. It also is home to a handful of world-famous art colonies, like those at Ogunquit and Monhegan. Works by famous artists are in many collections across Maine, and there are also a dozen or so fine galleries along the length of the coast where you might find as yet unknown masterpieces. Here are a few of the outstanding museums that make up the state's newly formed Maine Art Trail, as well as a handful of more unusual offerings.

🌲 **Bates College Museum of Art**. The prints, drawings, and paintings of Marsden Hartley, a Lewiston native, are featured in this collection, along with a variety of works by other well-known artists, including Alex Katz, Alan Bray, and Ann Lofquist. 75 Russell Street, Bates College, Lewiston (bates.edu/acad/museum).

🌲 **Bowdoin College Museum of Art**. Here you'll find one of the earliest collegiate collections in America, with art from ancient Greece, Rome, and Asia, as well as European and American works representing a broad time period. Walker Art Building, Bowdoin College, Brunswick (bowdoin.edu/art-museum).

🌲 **Colby College Museum of Art**. Twentieth-century American artists, including John Marin, Fairfield Porter, and George Bellows, are showcased here, along with a large collection of works by Alex Katz. The museum also features early portraiture by John Singleton Copley, Gilbert Stuart, and Charles Wilson (colby.edu/museum).

🌲 **Farnsworth Art Museum**. A focus on art created in or inspired by Maine has earned the Farnsworth recognition as one of the finest regional art museums in the country. Works by Fitz Henri Lane, Rockwell Kent, and Louise Nevelson are part of the Rockland museum's permanent collection, but the biggest attraction is the Wyeth Center, which boasts the world's largest collection of art by N. C., Andrew, and Jamie Wyeth (farnsworthmuseum.org).

🌲 **Jones Museum of Glass and Ceramics**. A unique and very respected museum in the world of glass, the Jones Museum in Sebago features more than seven thousand works in the permanent collection, plus a research library and gallery shop (35 Douglas Mountain Road, Sebago. 207-787-3370).

🌲 **Museum of African Tribal Art**. More than one thousand years of African history are represented in this world-class collection of tribal masks and artifacts in Portland (207-871-7188).

🌲 **Nowetah's American Indian Museum**. Genuine American Indian art from all parts of the United States, Canada, and South America, plus a collection of more than three hundred old Maine Indian sweetgrass/brown ash split baskets, are found in New Portland (207-628-4981).

🌲 **Portland Museum of Art**. The state's best-known museum has gained world renown with the gift of the Joan Whitney Payson Collection of Impressionist and Post-Impressionist works by Renoir, Degas, Monet, Picasso, and other masters. The heart of the museum is the State of Maine Collection, which features the work of such Maine artists as Winslow Homer, Edward Hopper, Rockwell Kent, John Marin, Maurice Prendergast, and Andrew Wyeth. Special exhibits and programs include a collection of fine and decorative arts dating from the nineteenth century to the present. The museum also hosts traveling exhibitions (portlandmuseum.org).

🌲 **University of Maine Museum of Art**. Highlights include works by Winslow Homer, Francisco Goya, and Pablo Picasso, as well as works on paper by David Hockney, Roy Lichtenstein, and Elizabeth Murray (umma.umaine.edu).

Music

The music scene in Maine is as lively a mix as can be found anywhere: chamber and choral groups, chanty singers, blues artists, fiddle players, rock bands, several orchestras, and a bevy of music festivals.

"Maine is incredibly vibrant musically," says Kathy Hammond of the Portland Symphony Orchestra. "There's a lot to do here, and a great variety of types of music, including folk, ethnic, and classical. Maine offers ways for music lovers to observe, and ample opportunities for musicians to play."

You might not suspect it, but there is a lively blues scene in Maine, as evidenced by the Maine Blues Society (mainebluessociety.com), scores of blues nights at pubs and bars, and annual blues festivals, including the Maine Blues Festival (held each June in Naples) and the North Atlantic Blues Festival (northatlanticbluesfestival.com) held each August in Rockland.

One of the newest venues in the state is Darling's Waterfront Pavilion, an open-air amphitheater located in a fifty-eight-acre public park along the banks of the Penobscot River in Bangor.

The Pavilion first opened in 2010 and was renamed in 2013 when a local car dealership stepped in to be a sponsor. A study that same year by the University of Maine showed that the economic impact of the concert series held since the Pavilion opened totaled more than $30 million. The Kahbang Music, Art, and Film Festival and the American Folk Festival are also held at Waterfront Park.

ORCHESTRAS

Maine has a number of orchestras, based in Augusta, the midcoast, southern Maine, and at university campuses around the state. And there are two professional symphonies: the Bangor Symphony Orchestra (BSO) and the Portland Symphony Orchestra (PSO).

The Bangor Symphony Orchestra's first performance was in November 1896, making the group the oldest continuously performing community orchestra in the United States. Today's performances are held at the Hutchins Concert Hall at the Maine Center for the Performing Arts in Orono, a venue with remarkable acoustics and not a bad seat in the house. The symphony is currently composed of ninety members, most of whom live within the state and have full- or part-time jobs in addition to their musical careers. (One is a lobsterman.) The BSO's conductor is Lucas Richman, who joined the orchestra in 2010. Favorite performances include Beethoven's Ninth Symphony, accompanied by a two hundred-voice chorus. For more information visit bangorsymphony.com.

Not quite as old but just as beloved, the ninety-two-year-old Portland Symphony Orchestra performs at Merrill Auditorium, home of the famous Kotzschmar Organ, one of the largest pipe organs in the world. The PSO is a $2.6-million orchestra, offering fifty-six full concerts each year under the direction of conductor Robert Moody. In addition, the group performs more than one hundred other programs, including Mozart & More, informal concerts celebrating the genius of Mozart. For lighter fare, the orchestra's pops concerts present offerings as diverse as swing dance music, Broadway hits, Hollywood favorites, and the familiar music of Rodgers and Hammerstein. For more information visit the PSO's Web site at portlandsymphony.com.

MORE MUSIC

- **Bay Chamber Concerts**. A series of classical music concerts have been held in the Rockport Opera House, winter and summer, in the midcoast community since 1961 (baychamberconcerts.org).
- **Cormorant Chamber Players of Maine**. A small but lively combo based in Boothbay Harbor (207-633-3936).
- **Center for the Arts at the Chocolate Church**. An eclectic mix of music (including folk) and theater is offered at this Bath landmark year-round (chocolatechurch.com).
- **Machias Bay Chamber Concerts**. Ensemble performances are held each summer in the historic Center Street Congregational Church in Machias (machiasbaychamberconcerts.com).
- **Maine Music Society**. The society presents the Androscoggin Chorale and Maine Chamber Ensemble in a series of choral and orchestral performances throughout the year. They also offer the Summer Chamber Music Series with educational outreach programs in the Lewiston/Auburn area (mainemusicsociety.org).

Opera

🌲 **The Gilbert and Sullivan Society of Maine**. Each year the society produces a Gilbert and Sullivan comic opera, six in winter and three in summer. The cast, crew, and orchestra are all volunteers from the Ellsworth area (gilbertsullivanmaine.org).

🌲 **Portland Opera Repertory Theatre (PORT)**. PORT performs in the newly refurbished Merrill Auditorium to sell-out crowds of opera fans. The past season's production was an elaborate performance of Puccini's *La Boheme* (portopera.org).

Dance

Many Mainers enjoy dancing, both as performers and as spectators. Grange halls host foot-stomping contra dances, folk dances, and square dances, and studios for jazz, ballet, tap, swing, ballroom, and African dancing are found around the state. Here are just a few of the many performance offerings.

🌲 **Maine State Ballet**. Established in 1986 and located in Portland, the Maine State Ballet has quickly become the leading professional dance company in the state. In cooperation with the Maine State School for the Performing Arts, the troupe educates, entertains, and enriches the community through varied dance programs, including full-length ballets and one-act productions. The company is accompanied by the Maine State Ballet Orchestra (mainestateballet.org).

🌲 **Robinson Ballet**. Headquartered in Bangor's River City Dance Center, the Robinson company has been delighting audiences for more than twenty years, including popular annual Christmas performances of *The Nutcracker* (robinsonballet.org).

🌲 **Swing and Sway**. Ballroom dance instruction by nationally recognized teachers in Rockland, featuring private lessons, group classes, shows, competitions, and social events (swingnsway.com).

Schools and Workshops

Want to try your hand at a new art form? Build a dory or a highboy? Maine is home to many quality programs for everything from language study to ceramics. Here are a few ideas.

🌲 **Atlantic Challenge**. Here's where you'll find highly respected boatbuilding courses along the shores of Penobscot Bay in Rockland (apprenticeshop.com).

🌲 **Center for Furniture Craftsmanship**. Founded in 1993, the center provides programs for novice, intermediate, and advanced woodworkers to hone their craft in a supportive environment in a pretty setting in Rockport (woodschool.org).

🌲 **Haystack Mountain School of Crafts**. A nationally known school on Deer Isle offering two- and three-week workshops in visual arts and craft media. Faculty work is on display periodically (haystack-mtn.org).

🌲 **The Landing School of Boatbuilding and Design**. A full-time vocational school, this southern Maine facility in Arundel offers courses in yacht design and boatbuilding (landingschool.org).

🌲 **Maine College of Art**. Right in the center of downtown, the Maine College of Art invigorates Portland's arts district with young and enthusiastic artists and a well-regarded faculty (meca.edu).

🌲 **Penobscot School**. The Penobscot School was founded in 1986 as a nonprofit language school and center for international exchange, and it has attracted people from around the world to the small city of Rockland. Programs include summer English immersion for adults from away, foreign language immersion weekends for Mainers and visitors, and weekly classes—from beginner to advanced—in many languages (penobscot.us).

🌲 **Maine Media Workshops**. Founded as the Maine Photographic Workshops, Maine Media has an international reputation for courses in both photography and film. Top Hollywood players often pick up tricks of the trade right here in the little village of Rockport (mainemedia.edu).

🌲 **Skowhegan School of Painting and Sculpture**. A famous arts institution for serious students (skowheganart.org).

🌲 **WoodenBoat School**. An offshoot of the authoritative *WoodenBoat* magazine, this Brooklin school is where dedicated aficionados go to build their dream vessel (woodenboat.com).

History Museums

Maine loves its rich history, as the number of history museums and historic buildings scattered across the state attest. These venerable institutions run the gamut from historic houses offering a well-preserved glimpse into the past to respected professional facilities with full-time staffs and research facilities. Some are open seasonally, so be sure to check before museum-hopping your way through the state. Here is a partial listing; for a complete list, check Maine Archives and Museums at mainmuseums.org.

- **Abbe Museum**. Located within Acadia National Park at Sieur de Monts Spring, this award-winning museum celebrates Maine's Native American heritage. Discover ten thousand years of culture, history, art, and archaeology through changing exhibits and workshops taught by Native American artists (abbemuseum.org).
- **Brick Store Museum**. A history and art museum focusing on southern Maine with changing exhibitions and a semipermanent exhibition on Kennebunk and the Federal period (brickstoremuseum.org).
- **Burnham Tavern Museum**. The tavern, built in 1770 in Machias, features Revolutionary War information and artifacts and is a National Historic Site. It was the staging point for the first naval battle of the war (burnhamtavern.com).
- **Center for Maine History**. Part of the Maine Historical Society campus on Congress Street in Portland, the center features more than eight thousand items and hosts large-scale annual exhibitions (mainehistory.org).
- **College of the Atlantic Natural History Museum**. The nature museum at this highly regarded ecology school in Bar Harbor features dioramas of animals and plants of Mount Desert Island, from foxes to finbacks (coa.edu).
- **Colonial Pemaquid**. A unique collection from the Colonial era, Colonial Pemaquid is a sort of in-the-field archaeological museum situated as it is alongside ongoing excavations (friendsofcolonialpemaquid.org).
- **Hudson Museum**. On the campus of the University of Maine, this unusual museum—an anthropology collection featuring pre-Columbian artifacts—wraps around the Maine Center for the Arts (umaine.edu/hudsonmuseum).
- **The Kittery Historical and Naval Museum**. The building of naval vessels in Kittery began during the Revolutionary War with the construction of John Paul Jones's sloop *Ranger* in 1777. The museum showcases a model of that vessel, plus artifacts galore depicting shipbuilding in the southernmost town in the state (kitterymuseum.com).

🌲 **Maine Folklife Center**. An up-and-comer on Maine's museum scene, the Folklife Center showcases the folklore and oral history of the state (umaine.edu/folklife/).

🌲 **Maine Forest and Logging Museum**. Just outside of Bangor in Leonard's Mills, this is a living-history museum, a 265-acre property on which a late eighteenth-century logging operation is recreated (leonardsmills.com).

🌲 **Maine State Museum**. Located in the Capitol Complex in Augusta, the Maine State Museum features very detailed exhibits on all aspects of the state's history and culture from its earliest days. Many states have state museums—this one has a reputation as being among the best. Open daily, year-round (mainestatemuseum. org).

🌲 **Moosehead Marine Museum**. The centerpiece of this upcountry, lakeside museum in Greenville is the restored steamer *Katahdin*, which offers cruises on the state's largest lake every summer (katahdincruises.com/Museum.php).

🌲 **Museum of Vintage Fashion**. A highly regarded collection of antique clothing in The County, open seasonally. Island Falls (207-862-3797).

🌲 **Patten Lumbermen's Museum**. An outstanding collection of artifacts of the lumbering era in the Maine woods, this museum includes more than three thousand artifacts displayed in nine buildings (lumbermensmuseum.org).

🌲 **Peary-MacMillan Arctic Museum**. This museum, on the campus of Bowdoin College, is filled with the photographs, diaries, and personal records of Admiral Robert Peary, the first man to reach the North Pole, and his assistant Donald MacMillan (bowdoin.edu/ arctic-museum).

🌲 **Pownalborough Courthouse**. Not far from Wiscasset, in the little town of Dresden, this is the oldest pre–Revolutionary War hall of justice in Maine (lincolncountyhistory.org).

🌲 **Shaker Museum**. Maine is home to the only remaining colony of Shakers, and this small museum in New Gloucester—right at their homestead—offers an excellent overview of life in a Shaker village (maineshakers.com).

🌲 **Thompson's Ice House**. Back when ice was an industry, Thompson's was a player. Now you can see ice cut the old-fashioned way at a site on the National Register of Historic Places in South Bristol (thompsonicehouse.com).

🌲 **Washburn-Norlands Living History Center**. Rural Maine life in the 1800s is relived on this 430-acre farm in Livermore. Try the ninety-minute guided tour (norlands.org).

🌲 **Woodlawn Museum**. Home of the Colonel Black Mansion, one of the few buildings in Maine that can rightly be called a mansion, this richly furnished Georgian-period home on 180 acres in Ellsworth is known for its gracious gardens (woodlawnmuseum.com).

Maritime Museums

Few places have as rich a seafaring legacy as does Maine, and the state displays its salty heritage proudly at a handful of institutions.

🌲 **Maine Maritime Academy**. While not exactly a museum, Maine Maritime Academy's training ship *State of Maine* is living history. Tour it and the Castine school, too (mainemaritime.edu).

🌲 **Maine Maritime Museum**. With its collections and exhibitions, this Bath museum interprets the role of Maine ships and sailors in national and international maritime affairs since 1607. The museum's centerpiece is the Maritime History Building, where an extensive collection of artifacts, ship models, portraits, photographs, and memorabilia is displayed. The thirty-thousand-square-foot building is adjacent to the restored Percy and Small Shipyard, which may be the only wooden shipbuilding yard from the nineteenth century still in existence in the United States. Once majestic four-, five-, and six-masted schooners were built here, and today, wooden boats are still crafted in the yard. The museum's excursion boat *Summertime* makes several cruises along the adjacent Kennebec River, adding a nice dimension to an entertaining and educational visit. Open year-round (mainemaritimemuseum.org).

🌲 **Penobscot Marine Museum**. Much of the seafaring activity that built this nation's early economy began in the Penobscot Bay region. This museum, right on Route 1 in Searsport, features a pristine collection of marine paintings, small craft, and artifacts that trace the history of boatbuilding in the area. The collections and exhibits are housed in eight historic structures, including the renovated Captain Jeremiah Merithew House, home to a fine collection of twenty-five marine paintings by noted artists James and Thomas Buttersworth. Both children and adults will enjoy the Fowler-True-Ross House, a nineteenth-century sea captain's home reflecting family life and the treasures brought back from many voyages. In the Nichols-Colcord-Duncan Barn, the museum's collection of recreational small craft and local fishing vessels are showcased (penobscotmarinemuseum.org).

🕯 **The Maine Lighthouse Museum**. The state's largest collection of lighthouse and Coast Guard artifacts are at this unique museum in Rockland. Items include rare lighthouse lenses, working lights, buoys, foghorns, bells, and lifesaving and lighthouse equipment. The museum also has lighthouse and ship models, a permanent exhibit of Civil War uniforms and weapons, and a Liewella Mills doll collection complete with costumes, from circa 1399 to 1890 (mainelighthousemuseum.com).

Transportation Museums

See an antique biplane zoom overhead, take a bumpy ride on a Model T, or feel the wind in your hair as a steam engine train chugs through the countryside. Maine has an extensive collection of transportation museums, with everything but lunar modules on display.

🕯 **Boothbay Railway Village**. A summer favorite in the Boothbay area, this museum is a miniature village and includes a fine collection of antique cars and a narrow-gauge railroad (railwayvillage. org).

🕯 **Cole Land Transportation Museum**. If it is an industrial vehicle that was once put to work in Maine, it can be found in this Bangor museum. A fine collection of antique trucks and accessories (colemuseum.org).

🕯 **Maine Narrow Gauge Railroad**. Narrow-gauge trains once crisscrossed Maine. The two-footers operated from rural areas, hauling slate, wood, and farm products to standard-gauge trains for shipment to markets around the world. The Trust for the Preservation of Maine Industrial History and Technology brought some of these vehicles back to Maine from the Edaville Railroad Museum in Massachusetts in 1993. Inside the museum are a 1913 locomotive, seven passenger cars, and much more (mainenarrowgauge. org).

🕯 **Maine Watercraft Museum**. One of the best-kept secrets in the midcoast area, this museum houses watercraft built prior to 1960. There are more than one hundred antique and classic craft on display, including Old Town canoes. Open seasonally in Thomaston (ohwy.com).

🌲 **Owls Head Transportation Museum**. An institution on the midcoast, this museum boasts one of the finest collections of landmark aircraft and pre-1930 vehicles to be found anywhere. Pioneer engines, automobiles, carriages, bicycles, and motorcycles are maintained in operating condition and demonstrated during weekend special events and airshows, attracting visitors from all around the Northeast. (Hundreds bring their own pre-1970 vehicles to exhibit.) Highlights include World War I fighter planes, the Red Baron's Fokker Triplane, and a full-scale replica of the Wright Brothers' famous 1903 flyer. Road machines include a 1914 Rolls-Royce Ghost limousine and a restored Model T bus ready for riders. Open all year (owlshead.org).

🌲 **Seal Cove Auto Museum**. This often overlooked collection features more than one hundred antique autos, including Edsels (sealcoveautomuseum.org).

🌲 **Seashore Trolley Museum**. More than two hundred transit vehicles, many operational, including MBTA trolleys, wooden cars from Europe, old New England horse-drawn cars, and much more are featured at this south coast institution in Kennebunkport (trolleymuseum.org).

🌲 **Stanley Museum**. This small museum features famous Stanley Steamer cars, invented by the twin brothers Stanley from right here in Kingfield. Also displayed are fascinating antique photographs by the Stanley's sister, Chansonetta Stanley Emmons, a pioneering shutterbug (stanleymuseum.org).

🌲 **Wells Auto Museum**. Some eighty restored autos, many of them built before 1915, including a large display of "Brass Era" antique cars, are housed here—after 1915, manufacturers turned from polished brass to painted headlamps, radiators, and trim (wellsautomuseum.com/collection).

Festivals and Fairs

Maine is the home of scores of wonderful celebrations. Some spotlight talented musicians, artists, and dancers, while others highlight the state's seafaring or agricultural heritage. Still others celebrate Maine's variety of cultures. Whatever the reason, if you're a fan of festivals or fairs, you're sure to find something to your liking. Here's a selection of offerings. For more information, see the Maine Tourism Association's calendar of events at mainetourism.com, or call them at 207-623-0363.

- **Acadian Festival**. Way up in The County in the St. John Valley, this annual June gathering celebrates the local French-Acadian culture through music (acadianfestival.com).
- **Annual Maine Indian Basket Makers Sale and Demonstration**. This December event takes place at the Hudson Museum on the University of Maine campus. It features Maliseet, Micmac, Passamaquoddy, and Penobscot craftspeople who sell their handmade, one-of-a-kind, ash splint and sweet grass basketry. Work baskets, such as creels, pack and potato baskets, and curly bowls may be found along with quill jewelry, wood carvings, and birch bark work. Traditional foods served up by the Indian Island Cafe, storytelling and flute music, and demonstrations of brown ash pounding are also presented (maineindianbaskets.org).
- **Common Ground Fair**. The Common Ground Fair is held each fall in late September to celebrate rural living. Sponsored by the Maine Organic Farmers and Gardener's Association, the fair is three days of music, displays, children's activities, and wonderfully tasty organic food in Unity. The sheep dog demonstrations are always popular (mofga.org).
- **La Kermesse Festival**. A four-day Franco-American festival held in late June in Biddeford, La Kermesse features a parade, a block party, and loads of entertainment (lakermessefestival.com).
- **Maine Lobster Festival**. A three-day extravaganza in Rockland held in early August featuring Maine's most famous crustacean. Highlights include a lively parade, big-name music acts, exhibits, and—you guessed it—pot after pot of steaming lobsters (mainelobsterfestival.com).
- **Maine Potato Blossom Festival**. Hooray for Maine's spuds! This July event includes the crowning of the Potato Blossom Queen, a pageant, mashed potato wrestling, fireworks, and the thrilling 'Roostook River Raft Race. In Fort Fairfield (207-472-3800).
- **The Moxie Festival**. A wacky and fun festival in Lisbon featuring crafts, a parade, entertainment, and carnival rides, this July staple honors the soft drink with the distinctive taste (moxiefestival.com).
- **North Atlantic Blues Festival**. Rockland gets rocking for a few days in July when nationally known blues artists show up and play (northatlanticbluesfestival.com).

🌲 **Thomas Point Beach Bluegrass Festival**. This shindig has enjoyed great popularity in recent years. It's held in early September in Brunswick and draws bluegrass fans from around the state—and many from away, too (thomaspointbeach.com).

🌲 **Topsham Fair**. One of Maine's largest agricultural fairs, this great festival is held annually in August. Thousands show up for farm-related displays, harness racing, crafts, and home cooking (topsham-fair.net).

🌲 **Yarmouth Clam Festival**. Bivalves get their day during mid-July; celebrated with a midway, parades, races, good eatin', and more (clamfestival.com).

🌲 **Union Fair and Blueberry Festival**. An old-fashioned agricultural fair with harness racing, pig scrambles, and a unique museum, plus a tasty festival celebrating Maine's tangy wild blueberry (union-fair.org).

Conferences

Maine is the site of several exciting annual conferences. The state's universities and college sponsor conferences on every imaginable topic, such as the annual Women in Leadership Conference—featuring Maine's most dynamic leaders from business, politics, and education—held at Thomas College in Waterville.

Maine is also the kind of place where a group of people—or an individual—can organize and start something really exciting. For example, in 1989 a small group of people interested in world affairs—many of them because they were once deeply involved in such things—decided to organize a conference in the midcoast area. The event drew residents as well as government officials from around the globe who came together to hear lectures and participate in discussions. So successful was The Camden Conference (camdenconference.org) that it has continued every February for more than twenty-five years.

More recently, the midcoast has seen the growing popularity of the Camden International Film Festival. Begun by then-recent college grad Ben Fowlie in 2004, the event brings documentary filmmakers and enthusiasts from around the globe to Camden and Rockland in late September for screenings of dozens of films. The critically acclaimed festival is now recognized as one of the top twelve documentary film events in the world.

"Many of the world's leading festivals take place in urban centers and we thought that by bringing the industry to a community with fewer distractions, we could create an environment where 100 percent of the focus could be on the craft of nonfiction storytelling," says Fowlie. "The model is not that new for the region when you look at PopTech and the Camden Conference. What we did focus on was ensuring that we had strong representation from regional universities and emerging artists.

"It's extremely supportive here," he adds, "and very reassuring knowing that there is a strong, loyal network from the local community."

9

FAMILY LIFE

"I look forward to a time when my career is in a place where I can get out of Los Angeles and find a nice small town like I grew up in to raise my family."

—Patrick Dempsey, actor, raised in Buckfield

BEST PLACE TO RAISE KIDS

When former Governor John Baldacci was in the U.S. House of Representatives, he spent eight years living and working in Washington, D.C. In public statements he explained that his family did not accompany him to Washington, D.C., but stayed in Maine "because, frankly, this was the best place to raise children." The former governor's assertion has been seconded numerous times by children's advocacy groups who applaud Maine's kid-friendly policies, safe streets and cities, clean air, and old-fashioned sense of community. "In Maine, my nine- and six-year-old girls can be comfortable being kids," says Lynda Chilton, who moved to the state from Virginia. "Having fun can mean chasing frogs all afternoon, or going to the corner shop with friends for ice cream. They can walk home from school or go to the library without parental supervision. In Virginia, children were becoming mini grown-ups, with stresses and peer pressures that I didn't face when I was little."

Not that there aren't some stresses and pressures that children face here, the most serious of which is scarcity. According to the Annie E. Casey Foundation, 21 percent of Maine children are now living in poverty, the highest percentage in New England. Vermont, Connecticut, and Massachusetts have among the fewest poor children in poverty in the country, with 15 percent each.

Experts say that even more significantly, Maine's current figure is almost double what it was in 2001, when just 11 percent of the state's children were living in poverty.

They cite the growing cost of living and the fact that for years parents were able to brace against child care costs by sending a second parent into the workforce as reasons for the increase. It's a serious problem, and one that Maine's agencies most closely involved with children and families are working hard to address.

Prevention programs for problems such as substance abuse, youth violence, and teen pregnancy have shown great progress in Maine. In recent years, the state has been able to claim:

- The lowest infant mortality rate in the nation.
- The highest immunization rate in the nation.
- The third-lowest teen birthrate in the nation.
- The highest rate (90 percent) of women receiving prenatal care in the nation.
- The lowest number of families currently on public assistance since 1970.

More serious concerns aside, there is something magical about Maine and children. Think back to your childhood. Can you remember what mattered most to you? I have always loved roaming beaches, tromping through the woods, and spying on wildlife while canoeing on a quiet lake—fragments of time spent with family members in special, unhurried places. Maine is made for family recreation, for fun times that don't need to wait for a vacation.

Another special quality of life in Maine is the small-town atmosphere. Children are enriched by the community connections—the very real knowledge that grown-ups other than your parents know you, care about you, and will tell on you if you don't look when crossing the street. "Children have more freedom here," says Ruth Anne Hohfeld. "But if they act up, someone they know will call their parents."

And snow. What child doesn't find the phenomenon of snowflakes swirling down to earth a marvelous, miraculous event? (Not to mention the chance to miss school.)

"Jason and I moved to Maine because of family ties, but also because we wanted to raise our kids in a place that was safe, normal, beautiful, and full of good folks," says Kristy Scher.

Maine is that place.

PROFILE—A BETTER QUALITY OF LIFE

Central New Jersey was the home of Guy and Cherie Scott before they moved to Boothbay in 2008. "Our daughter was only ten months old and we didn't want her growing up in the hustle and bustle of the Tri-State area while we worked one hundred plus hours a week," explains Cherie. "We were disoriented with the lack of community spirit in our town and the high property taxes. We also were not thrilled with the idea of our daughter spending forty or more hours in a daycare while we worked at maximum capacity to afford the rising taxes and our home. We were craving a work-life balance, but New Jersey just couldn't afford us that privilege. Don't get me wrong: we still work hard in Maine, but we enjoy a higher quality of life and a consistent work-life balance."

The Scotts had a strange experience when they first moved up. "My husband would wake every summer morning to a low rumble. It drove him crazy, especially since we were so grateful to have moved as far as we could from the Jersey turnpike's noise and traffic. One morning, totally miffed, he went to see who was running a machine every morning. It turned out to be a lobsterman checking his traps at the dock below." The discovery came as a relief to Guy Scott. "It actually put a smile on my face each morning," he says. "What a charming way to wake up!"

KIDS AND SAFETY

According to Maine law, all passengers in a moving car must be buckled up. As far as adults are concerned, the seat belt law is a secondary law, which means a vehicle cannot be stopped just because a police office suspects the driver isn't wearing a seat belt. Where children are involved, however, the law is tougher. All kids nineteen years old and under must be strapped into their safety belts, and since this law is mandatory, drivers can be pulled over for not obeying it.

In 2003, Maine's Child Safety Seat Law got tougher. The new regulations state that children four years of age and younger must be in an approved child safety seat. A child who weighs less than forty pounds and who is less than four years of age must ride in a child safety seat. A child who weighs at least forty pounds but less than eighty pounds and who is less than eight years of age must ride in a federally approved child restraint system, such as a Booster Seat or a EZ-On Harness/Vest. A child who is less than twelve years of age and who weighs less than one hundred pounds must be properly secured in the back seat of the vehicle, if possible. As for bicycles, kids sixteen and under must wear bicycle helmets when riding their bikes.

Health Care

State-of-the-art birthing centers are found in Maine's hospitals, with certified nurse midwives and doula services the norm. For serious pediatric concerns, the Barbara Bush Children's Hospital at Maine Medical Center offers a comprehensive array of services for children, including the inpatient unit and other services throughout the hospital and beyond. Other facilities around the state have pediatric wings, such as Eastern Maine Medical Center in Bangor, which boasts a brand-new twenty-four-bed children's wing.

Adoption

Portland-based Stepping Stones is a full-service nonprofit international and domestic adoption agency that has placed more than four thousand children since 1977. Through their State Agency Adoption Program, they work to place as many infants and children living in state-run foster care as possible. Visit their Web site at www.steppingstonesusa.org. You might also visit Maine's Office of Child and Family Services at maine.gov/dhhs/ocfs. There you'll find profiles of Maine children awaiting adoptions as well as a guide to adoption in the state.

SCHOOLS

Education is among any parent's top concerns when relocating to a new community. "We were really concerned about schools for Alex," says Jan

Njaa of Belfast. "After talking with a school administrator and some parents we felt that Belfast would be a great place for her. We've been told there is a lack of activities for older kids, but we'll tackle that as it comes."

Maine has a progressive education system that is ranked among the top ten in the country. In recent years, the National Educational Goals Panel recognized Maine as the state with the highest performance in the nation in improving public education. Among the strengths of Maine's schools are small class size (the average is fourteen students per teacher), high student engagement, and high parental involvement. Communities tend to be concerned about—and involved in—what goes on within the school's doors.

"Just after we moved here from Chicago, our daughter's elementary school was threatened with consolidation," says Jan Njaa. "The community voiced their concern and we were impressed with how much the parents and neighbors valued having the schools in the neighborhood. The building will be renovated instead. There's a real sense of community in Maine, and we feel like the quality of the education Alex will get will be high."

In 2013, the Maine School Performance Grading System was launched to help people like Jan Njaa understand how well their children's schools are performing and what is being done to improve them. The rating system is based on several factors and uses a familiar A to F scale to provide a starting point. Student achievement in reading and math, the growth of the bottom 25 percent of students (for elementary schools), and the graduation rate (for high schools) are all factors that are taken into account. Although not everyone feels that the grading system deserves an "A," supporters argue that it brings transparency and accountability to school performance across the state and contains constructive information on the variables that most impact Maine student achievement, including student poverty, teacher tenure and education levels, and funding.

For specific information on individual schools, see the Maine Department of Education's Web site at maine.gov/education/index.shtml.

Educational Assessment

When Maine educators and parents want to improve learning, define teacher training needs, update classroom curriculum, or measure who's mastering the metric system, they turn to a set of standards called the Maine Learning Results. Revised in 2007, they reflect the knowledge and skills essential for college, careers, and civic life in the twenty-first century, and they have been updated to include the Common Core State Standards in English language arts and mathematics.

The Learning Results work in tandem with the Maine Comprehensive Assessment System (MeCAS), a combination of standardized tests that inform teaching and learning, measure students' mastery of Maine's academic standards and English language proficiency, and serve as the tool for holding schools accountable for student learning and English language acquisition.

So comprehensive are the Maine Learning Results that they address even nonacademic subjects such as gym. To help fight rising obesity rates among children, the Department of Education developed several innovative initiatives to help schools create a healthy nutrition and physical activity environment. One of the first steps has been to create the Learning Results Standards for Physical Education—a blueprint for assessing the physical well-being of Maine students.

School Organization

Schools in Maine are under local control. Some towns and cities supervise their own schools individually, others combine and pool educational resources in school administrative districts (S.A.D.s) or community school districts (C.S.D.s). "Kids do not seem to socialize with friends from school as much as I expected," says Betsy Biemann, who moved from New York City. "Here, social networks seem to be focused more on your neighbors and other networks. But that is an artifact in part of how Brunswick schools are organized—each of the four elementary schools draws kids from different parts of town so not all of their classmates live nearby."

Paula Palakawong's child is at Lincolnville Central School, a kindergarten-through-eighth-grade school in Waldo County, and she is impressed with the student-teacher ratio as well as equipment. "Each child has their own laptop and iPad, and this is in a town of only two thousand people. I have friends in Connecticut whose kid's schools aren't as well supplied."

Most Maine schools are supervised by a school board or committee, which administers education through a superintendent of schools. See the Department of Education's Web site for a complete list of school districts.

State-Funded Schools

Maine has five charter schools, as well as a new virtual charter school that opened in September of 2014, and the Maine School of Science and Mathematics, a public, residential high school in Limestone. The Governor Baxter School for the Deaf and the Arthur E. Gould School in South Portland are also state funded.

Private Schools

There are more than one hundred approved private schools in Maine, everything from Montessori schools to Waldorf to parochial schools. A few of these—like Lincoln Academy in the Damariscotta-Newcastle area— serve as public schools for local towns, which pay tuition for students. Size of student body varies: the Hilltop School in Bangor has only eighteen students, while Fryeburg Academy provides education for 530.

Arts in the Schools

L/A Arts, an outfit that brings world-class talent to the twin cities of Lewiston and Auburn, sponsors an innovative program that puts performers and artists into the schools on a regular basis. So popular is the program that it has been copied in communities around Maine and served as a model for similar programs in other states.

Betsy Biemann has found a "wonderful, and very inexpensive program for kids in art, swimming, and other after-school and weekend activities," in the midcoast area as well.

CHALLENGES STILL TO BE MET

There are family issues in Maine that need work, problems that the state and local communities are working hard to solve. "We've found so many plusses to living here," say Gordon and Carol Doherty-Cox of Port Clyde. "On the negative side, we were astonished at the amount of domestic abuse." Another newcomer, Gary Swanson, makes this observation: "Maine seems to have its share of dysfunctional individuals and families."

Maine has looked the problem of domestic abuse squarely in the eye and is taking steps to deal with it. In 2006, Governor Baldacci signed the first law in the country that gives judges the authority to protect pets when domestic abuse victims seek a protection order. "Maine is once again leading the nation by putting its people first," the governor said. The landmark law not only gives judges the power to include Spot and Fluffy on a protection from abuse order, but also gives them authority to impose penalties if the order is violated.

Combating domestic violence has been a personal cause for current Governor Paul LePage. In 2013, he issued an executive order establishing a new task force to address domestic violence and signed a law to develop and implement an electronic pilot project for electronic monitoring of certain domestic violence abusers. Governor LePage has also directed monies to the Maine Coalition to End Domestic Violence from his contingency fund and championed successful efforts to amend Maine's bail code to ensure judges determine bail for domestic violence offenses.

KID-FRIENDLY ACTIVITIES

"My kids can do all of the activities they did in Virginia and more," says Lynda Chilton. The Chilton family relocated to the midcoast after lots of research and years of looking for the best place to raise their children. "I wanted to make sure my family would not sacrifice anything from changing locations," explains Lynda. "I researched housing costs, available activities such as horseback riding and ballet, public and private schools, and business technology such as Internet access, multiple phone lines, and delivery services."

With information in hand, Lynda and her husband, Thad, realized they had no major concerns about relocating. "From visits here, we knew we loved the beauty and people of Maine," says Lynda. "We love the outdoors, and we enjoy real winters. The hard part became leaving my parents in Virginia who lived only a few minutes away." Fortunately, Lynda's parents visited often and eventually bought a second home in Maine themselves. "People should think about what they really like to do and see if they can keep doing those things in Maine," suggests Lynda. "Most of Maine is small-town living, and that has a character all its own."

Dance classes, music lessons, art workshops, Kindermusik—Maine has it all, in a setting that is conducive to quality family time. In addition to the offerings listed in chapter 7, here are a few more activities specifically for the young and young-at-heart.

Theater

Theater for children ranges from the many puppetry groups to several troupes in which kids are cast in starring roles. Best known of these is the Children's Museum and Theatre of Maine, headquartered in Portland, which features year-round productions, plus a comedy troupe and impro-visational classes. For more information, visit kitetails.org.

Museums

Maine is home to several museums that offer children insight into the state's rich history, art, and culture. The Children's Museum and Theatre of Maine, mentioned above, has three floors of interactive exhibits, and other museums are listed in chapter 8. Here are a few more specifically geared to the younger set.

- **Children's Discovery Museum.** Hands-on opportunities for children through grade five in Augusta (childrensdiscoverymuseum. org).
- **Maine Discovery Museum.** Offers indoor fun for children and located in downtown Bangor (mainediscoverymuseum.org).
- **Western Maine Play Museum.** A brand-new family learning center providing exhibits which encourage child/adult interaction in Wilton (westernmaineplay.org).

Music

Gifted musicians abound in Maine, ready to instruct your child in his or her instrument of choice. In addition to lessons, though, there are re-markable concert series designed just for children. Here are a few options:

- **KinderKonzerts.** These concerts by members of the Portland Symphony Orchestra bring live chamber music to preschool kids in Maine and New Hampshire. The children are introduced to the different families of orchestral instruments and the elements of music through audience participation, exciting demonstrations, and narration (portlandsymphony.org).
- **Portland Youth Concerts.** Held at Merrill Auditorium, these Portland Symphony Orchestra concerts introduce children ages seven through thirteen to the full symphony orchestra (port-landsymphony.org).
- **Bangor Youth Concerts.** The magic of live orchestral mu-sic—courtesy of the Bangor Symphony—is brought to more than four thousand school children from across the state. A highlight of each concert is a solo performance by the winner of the Bangor

Symphony Orchestra's Maine High School Concerto Competition (bangorsymphony.org).

🌲 **The Bangor Symphony Youth Orchestra and Ensemble**. The BSO Youth Orchestra provides an opportunity for student musicians to play orchestral music of a quality unmatched by school programs and private instruction. The orchestra inspires the musicians' confidence, challenges their musical abilities, and brings together peers who enjoy playing orchestral compositions (bangorsymphony.org).

🌲 **New England Music Camp**. A family-run music camp begun in Sidney in 1937, New England Music Camp offers quality and intensive musical education with popular sports and recreational activities. A sort of summer camp with horns (nemusiccamp.com).

Scouting and 4-H

Scouting for boys and girls is popular in the Pine Tree State, probably because of the many prime areas for top-notch outdoor activities. Hiking, tenting, canoeing, and swimming are all within a stone's throw for most scouts, and beautiful camping areas—some owned by the scouting councils—abound. The Pine Tree Council BSA oversees Boy Scouting in Maine. To contact the council, try their Web site at pinetreebsa.org. For Girl Scout information, contact girlscoutsofmaine.org.

Maine is also home to an active 4-H community, in which youngsters do such projects as raise livestock, make clothing, or grow vegetables. They then exhibit their efforts at fairs around the state. In Maine, 4-H is the youth development program of the University of Maine cooperative extension. For more information, see their Web site at umaine.edu/4h.

Summer Camps

Thousands of children from across the country come to camp in Maine every summer. They roast marshmallows, learn the breaststroke, and laugh and sing in their platform tents until they absolutely cannot keep their eyes open. They make friendships that may last for years, and learn skills that stand them in good stead into adulthood.

Many of the nation's first summer camps were founded in Maine, and some are still run by second- and third-generation camp directors. Dr. Luther H. Gulick, one of the founders of the Camp Fire Girls, started several of Maine's first camps, and championed the idea that summer camps should provide both educational and recreational activities. For more information on children's summer camps, see the Maine Office of Tourism's list at visitmaine.com.

Forts

What kid doesn't love a fort? Fortunately, Maine's got plenty. Here are a few to explore, but for more ideas, directions, and links to individual forts, see travel-maine.info/historic_forts for a very thorough list.

- **Fort Edgecomb**. This octagonal blockhouse has beautiful picnicking grounds overlooking the Sheepscot River in Edgecomb (207-882-7777).
- **Fort Halifax**. This fort's blockhouse was built in 1754 and is the oldest in the United States. Located in Winslow.
- **Fort Kent**. This blockhouse was erected in 1840 as part of military preparations for what looked like an impending war against Canada (207-941-4014).
- **Fort Knox Historical Site**. Perhaps the midcoast's best-known fort, Fort Knox, in Prospect, was built in 1844 to protect citizens from the British, and it has underground passages that never fail to intrigue children (207-469-7719).
- **Old Fort Western Museum**. A restored sixteen-room garrison house from 1755, Old Fort Western is in Augusta and is listed as a National Historic Landmark. It's the best field trip I ever chaperoned! (207-626-2385).
- **Fort William Henry**. Fort William Henry in Bristol is a replica of a colonial fort with fantastic views across Pemaquid Harbor (207-677-2423).
- **Fort Williams**. A very popular park in Greater Portland, Fort Williams has extensive grounds as well as some ruins that are fun to explore.

Animals

- **The Maine Wildlife Park**. This park, managed by the Department of Inland Fisheries and Wildlife, is home to injured or orphaned animals such as bear, deer, lynx, and even a mountain lion. The park is located in Gray (207-657-4977 or state.me.us/ifw/education/wildlifepark).

Maine Foods and Farms

One of the benefits of life in a rural state is the opportunity to visit working farms and orchards. Below are just a few places around the state where you can pick just about anything from blueberries to bush beans. More than one hundred pick-your-own farms open themselves to visitors, so for a complete list, check out Get Real Maine, a site sponsored by the Maine Department of Agriculture, Conservation, and Forestry, at getreal-maine.com.

- **Alheri Gardens**. Create bouquets from this Greater Portland farm's lovely gardens. Daffodils, tulips, peonies, and summer annuals are all available. Gray (207-657-4358).
- **Simons Hancock Farm**. Pick-your-own peas, beans, and pumpkins. Come fall, the farm offers hayrides to the pumpkin field, a big pumpkin smash, pumpkin weight guessing, and other games and amusements. Hancock (207-667-1359).
- **Dot Rupert's Strawberry Farm**. Tasty home of strawberries, raspberries, and highbush blueberries in the foothills of the western mountains. Hebron (207-966-2721).
- **Boutilier's Vegetables**. Pick-your-own vegetables way up in The County, including peas, beans, corn, tomatoes, carrots, beets, beet greens, and cucumbers. Benedicta (207-757-8312).

Apple Orchards

Of the forty orchards listed with the Maine Department of Agriculture, thirty-two are classified as pick-your-own. Some even offer kids the chance to visit farm animals, see a cider press, or take a hayride. Here is a sampling:

- **The Apple Farm**. Pumpkins, squash, cider, and apples ripe for the picking are the attraction here in Fairfield (lakesideorchards.com).
- **County Fair Farm**. This Lincoln County farm has a full farm stand, a baby animal barn, and weekend hayrides. Jefferson (207-549-3536).
- **Lemieux's Orchards**. Cider is made right here at the orchard, and you'll find loads of apple varieties. North Vassalboro (207-873-4354).
- **Merrill Apple Farms**. Look for the cider press and other produce in addition to all the apples. Ellsworth (207-667-4028).

🌲 **Spiller Farm**. Lots of varieties of apples await at this southern Maine farm in Wells, plus hayrides, strawberries, and garden veggies (spillerfarm.com).

MAINE MAPLE SUNDAY

Every March the state celebrates one of spring's sweetest rites—the making of maple syrup. Sugar makers open the doors of their sugarhouses to demonstrate just how maple sap is turned into everyone's favorite pancake topper. Many offer a variety of other treats and activities, including syrup on pancakes or ice cream, sugarbush tours, sleigh or wagon rides, and lots more. Maine Maple Sunday is always the fourth Sunday in March. For a list of participating sugarhouses, see mainemapleproducers.com.

10

JOINING THE COMMUNITY

"People don't use their front doors and being allowed to visit in the kitchen means you are part of the community."

—Ruth Anne Hohfeld, Rockland resident

How can you nourish your soul in Maine? Besides spending time enjoying nature, new residents find there are all kinds of community organizations that need and welcome participation. "There's plenty of opportunity for 'volunteer' employment," says Allie Lou Richardson of Islesboro. "I had worried that I was leaving all my friends, my church, and my community activities behind, but there's plenty to do, and welcoming, friendly people to do it with."

Many new residents find they enjoy giving back to their adopted communities through donating their time at service organizations, churches, and nonprofit groups. Still others train to become volunteer firefighters, docents at local museums, or directors on the board of the community YMCA. There are opportunities to mentor youth, maintain hiking trails, and care for wildlife. Once you've settled in a bit, town committees are another option for interested residents who want to see the inner workings of town politics.

"In our first year in Maine we met people and became involved in the community in a way that we hadn't imagined," says Kathleen Hirsch. "We took courses, attended concerts, volunteered, joined a health club, enjoyed hiking, kayaking, and the list goes on and on."

Perhaps you enjoy ornamental or vegetable gardening. Each year, it seems, more and more Mainers spend their spare time enriching the soil and cultivating beautiful blooms. "I was told people don't garden much in Maine," says Jan Njaa of Belfast. "But now that I live here, I see that's clearly not the case." In spite of (or perhaps because of) a short growing season, Mainers love their gardens and enjoy ready access to a variety of services that support green thumbs. In addition, an ever-increasing number of farmers' markets have sprouted in all corners of the state, providing high-quality, delicious produce as well as inspiration.

SPIRITUAL LIFE

"I'm surprised we've become so involved in church since moving to Maine," says Lynda Chilton. "We attended services in Virginia, but never were really a part of it. Here, it seems the churches are more integrated into the community."

Maine is a place of many faiths, too numerous to list completely. There are Presbyterian, Methodist, Congregational, Episcopalian, and Catholic churches along with Quaker Meeting Houses and Jewish synagogues. Many communities have Baptist and Unitarian-Universalist churches, and eight communities around the state have mosques. Other Eastern religions, while in the minority, are slowly growing. Most Maine congregations—regardless of faith—are small by city standards.

Historically, the religious group that goes back the farthest in Maine is Congregationalism, a Protestant denomination. Many of the state's most historic buildings are United Church of Christ churches, built a century or so ago for town meeting halls as well as places of worship. There are approximately 175 active Congregational Churches in Maine today, including the First Parish Congregational in Brunswick, where Martin Luther King, Jr., once preached and Harriet Beecher Stowe regularly worshipped.

Maine's Roman Catholic population grew rapidly with the influx of Irish immigrants in the early 1800s, and then, following the Civil War, with the large numbers of French Canadians who came to work in the mills. Today, about one-quarter of Maine's people are Roman Catholic, worshipping in 191 churches ranging from large cathedrals, such as Lewiston's stunning Saints Peter and Paul Church, to tiny missions whose visiting parish priests travel by ferry.

The Jewish community in Maine is small but active. There are approximately twenty synagogues in the state, with more than five hundred families at Portland's Temple Beth El alone. Beth El, located on Deering Avenue, also has a Hebrew school with more than 140 pupils.

Meditation, mindfulness, spiritual healing—you'll find it all in Maine, along with yoga disciplines, Shamanic journeying, and Zen meet-up groups. In coastal Northport, you can even attend a session with a medium at Temple Heights, the oldest operating spiritualist camp in the country, whose doors first opened during America's Gilded Age in 1882 (temple-heightscamp.org).

THE VOLUNTEERMAINE PARTNERSHIP

Here's another example of how Mainers break new ground with innovative thinking. Established in 2003, VolunteerMaine is a collaborative partnership between United Ways in Maine and the Maine Commission for Community Service to promote volunteerism. Originally run by the State Planning Office, the program links volunteers with organizations, both locally and out of state, seeking help through a statewide Web-based volunteer database—the first of its kind in the nation. Recent listings seek volunteers to rake leaves for seniors, to winterize homes for low-income residents, and to drive to Boston to retrieve dogs displaced by tropical storms. Check out their Web site at volunteermaine.org to see which organizations need you!

SERVICE ORGANIZATIONS

Maine men and women can get involved in a wide range of service organizations, from Rotary International to the American Association of University Women. Here is what's available, for example, in Hancock County alone:

American Legion	Daughters of the American
Rotary International	Revolution
Elks Club	League of Women Voters
Kiwanis Club	Kiwanis Club
Lions Club	Lioness Club
Peace, International	Women's Literary Club
	Zonta Club

To research which groups can be found in individual communities, contact area chambers of commerce listed in the back of the book.

NONPROFIT ORGANIZATIONS

In addition to service clubs, scores of nonprofit groups assist causes ranging from protecting Maine's islands to helping victims of AIDS. Maine has branches of national organizations, such as Habitat for Humanity and the Make-A-Wish Foundation, as well as nonprofits that are specific to the state.

For example, Maine Island Trail Association volunteers manage recreational use of about eighty public and private islands along more than three hundred miles of coast. Based in Rockland and Portland, the organization was set up to encourage thoughtful, low-impact use of Maine islands. The association depends on volunteers, as do so many worthwhile groups. Again, your local chamber of commerce will know what groups are in your area. If you'd like more information on the Maine Island Trail Association, see their Web site at mita.org.

RETIRED SENIOR VOLUNTEER PROGRAM (RSVP)

The RSVP program, part of Senior Corps and administered by the Corporation for National and Community Service, matches volunteers aged fifty-five and older with community service jobs such as delivering meals, providing companionship to homebound individuals, and teaching in literacy programs. RSVP volunteers also serve at the Maine State Museum and in local schools, libraries, nursing homes, and hospitals. For more information, see the Web site for VolunteerMaine at volunteermaine.org.

SERVICE CORPS OF RETIRED EXECUTIVES (SCORE)

This organization of volunteers, which is supported by the U.S. Small Business Administration (SBA), recruits retired executives who are interested in utilizing their past experience to counsel people who are starting up small businesses. Volunteers receive travel expenses. For more information, see their Web site at score.org. There you can type in your zip code to find the chapter nearest you.

MAINE SENIOR GAMES

Held in Portland and Bangor, the Maine Senior Games are the state's largest organized competitive event for the over-age-forty-five members of the population. For information about how you can have fun (and stay fit) by competing in the games, check the Southern Maine Agency on Aging's Web site at smaaa.org.

GARDENING

Nourishing the soil is another way to nourish one's soul. "If you can garden in Maine, you can garden anywhere," was the old slogan of *People, Places, and Plants*, a gardening magazine featuring the state established in 1996 in Gray and published until 2009. Maine's four growing zones, a frost-free season of—in some years—only one hundred days, and its notoriously rocky soil might lead people from outside the state to doubt that anything can grow here. What's going to bloom in a place with chilly springs and short—albeit glorious—summers?

The truth is that Maine has a dynamic horticultural scene, with first-rate ornamental gardening and an exploding organic vegetable market. Farming is taking off, too, as millennials who yearn to get back to the land find that Maine is one of the few New England states with affordable farmland.

The secret to gardening successfully, say veterans, is picking the right plants. Varieties of just about anything you might wish to grow are hardy in Maine—even tender vegetables such as eggplant and artichoke. Gardening pros cite the University of Maine's Horticultural Department as a huge asset to the state's gardeners, as well as Johnny's Selected Seeds, in Albion, a company with extensive trial gardens and thousands of varieties of plants. Extensive testing and research is going on right here in Maine, helping recreational and professional gardeners alike to choose plants that work well.

Other resources available to gardeners include the University of Maine Cooperative Extension Service, part of an amazing federal network that exists to impart free or low-cost agricultural information to the public. Check out their Web site at umaine.edu to find an office near you, or to take their questionnaire to determine whether you've got what it takes to be a farmer.

And then there are your neighbors, or vendors at the local farmers' market, who invariably seem to know the answers to gardening questions.

The length of the growing season can vary in Maine. Depending on where in the state you garden, you may have a slightly longer growing season and warmer temperatures. Luck is another factor. Killing frosts don't always arrive when the calendar says autumn. Some years bring mild autumns, with gardens blooming from the first of May until mid-October.

Many gardeners extend the season by protecting against early frosts, or using cold frames and the like to get an earlier jump on spring.

Gardening in Maine has its distinct advantages. For one thing, blooms are more brilliant, due to the cooler temperatures and intensity of the growing period. Another bonus is that many pests that plague gardeners in warmer climes can't survive the chilly winters. The cool summer nights are a boon to many plant varieties, and pleasant daytime temperatures and usually reliable rains mean spare time isn't spent watering. Probably the biggest advantage to gardening here, though, is the anticipation of and excitement during the growing season.

"Perhaps because the time is short, Mainers throw themselves into gardening," says Paul Tukey, who founded *People, Places, and Plants*. The quality, quantity, and breathtaking beauty of Maine's gardens is a testament to the talent and dedication of the state's gardeners, many of whom dream away the worst of winter days with dreams of digging in the dirt come spring.

FARMERS' MARKETS

The one hundred or so farmers' markets in Maine forge a direct link between consumers and farmers, which means unparalleled freshness. Markets are located in convenient spots throughout the state, and each offers a unique blend of personalities and products. Many operate inside during the winter as well!

Two markets are featured below, but to find the ones nearest you, check out the Get Real Maine Web site, sponsored by the Department of Agriculture, Conservation and Forestry at www.getrealmaine.com, or see the Maine Federation of Farmers' Markets at mainefarmersmarkets.org.

- **Belfast Farmers' Market**. Located at the Waterfall Arts gallery at 256 High Street, the market features the Bread Box Bakery, Mainely Poultry, and Field of Greens, in addition to other farmers and vendors. Open May through October on Friday from 9:00 a.m. to 1:00 p.m., with a change of location and hours come winter (belfastfarmersmarket.org).
- **Orono Farmers' Market**. Located between College Avenue and the Stillwater River, less than a mile from downtown Orono, at the University Steam Plant parking lot, the Orono market features local produce, maple syrup, jams and jellies, and local crafts. Open every

Saturday morning and Tuesday afternoon, May through October, rain or shine (oronofarmersmarket.org).

PUBLIC GARDENS

Mainers show their enthusiasm for growing things at the close to one hundred public gardens maintained by garden clubs and other organizations, including Coastal Maine Botanical Gardens, a spectacular 270-acre botanical garden in Boothbay that is fast gaining in stature and world-class recognition (mainegardens.org). Beautiful in any season, the gardens feature a Children's Garden and, my favorite—a Garden of the Five Senses.

In Maine, you can view Victorian-era horticulture at Hamilton House Gardens in South Berwick, or see Christina's Garden at the Olson House in Cushing, the subject of Andrew Wyeth's classic American painting. Escape summer crowds in a classically designed garden by Fletcher Steele at the Camden Amphitheater, or tour Johnny's Selected Seeds, home to America's most extensive trial gardens, in Albion. If you want gardening inspiration, you can find it in Maine!

The Garden Club Federation of Maine has a list of more than ninety gardens in alphabetical order on their Web site at mainegardenclubs.org, available in a printable spreadsheet format that you can take with you garden-hopping.

PROFILE—JUST COULDN'T STAY AWAY

The second edition of *Moving to Maine* contained a profile of Polly and Bob Knapp, who were reluctantly selling their vacation home in Maine. They vowed they would return . . . and they have!

"The birth of our first grandchild in 2006 prompted us to sell our home in Maine and move to Asheville, North Carolina, to be closer to her," explains Polly. "As she has gotten older, she's become more and more involved in after-school activities and summer camps. Spending time with her was becoming less and less. Any grandparents out there can understand I'm sure." Polly says that while the mountains of western North Carolina are beautiful,

"Maine kept tugging at my heart. I missed the beauty of the shore-line and the islands beyond, as well as the wonderful friends we'd made when we lived here." In 2014, the Knapps purchased another vacation home in Maine. "We are on our way back to 'The Way Life Should Be,' and possibly permanently. At our age, why not live in the place you love? As my husband says, 'There is nothing better than eating lobster on the deck at the Waterfront restaurant, waking up to three feet of snow on Christmas morning, or eating Christmas dinner at the Samoset or the Youngtown Inn." Polly chuckles and adds, "You know where his thoughts are—lobstah!"

APPENDIX 1

Maine at a Glance

Data provided by *Down East* magazine.

County	Androscoggin	Aroostook	Cumberland	Franklin
Population 2004★	107,022	73,390	273,505	29,736
Population 1990	105,259	86,936	243,135	29,008
Population 1980	99,509	91,344	215,789	27,447
Largest Town (2000 pop.)	Lewiston 35,690	Presque Isle 9,511	Portland 64,249	Farmington 7,410
People per Square Mile	220.8	11.1	317.7	17.4
High School Graduates	79.8%	76.9%	90.1%	85.2%
College/Adv. Degree	12.6%	12.5%	27.6%	17.7%
Median Household Income	$35,793	$28,837	$44,048	$31,459
Aver. Temp. Range, °F	Lewiston	Caribou	Portland	Farmington
January	29.2 to 11.1	19.4 to −1.6	30.3 to 11.4	25.8 to 0.5
April	53.1 to 34.2	46.7 to 29	52.3 to 34.1	51 to 28.5
July	80.7 to 60.7	76.5 to 54.5	78.8 to 58.3	73 to 53.4
October	59 to 40.5	52 to 34	58.7 to 38.3	57.4 to 32.3
Crime Rate per Thousand (2000)	35.79	20.61	30.23	31.81

★Most recent census estimate.

County	Hancock	Kennebec	Knox	Lincoln
Population 2004★	53,556	120,645	41,008	35,236
Population 1990	46,948	115,904	36,310	30,357
Population 1980	41,781	109,889	32,941	25,691
Largest Town	Ellsworth	Augusta	Rockland	Waldoboro
(2000 pop.)	6,456	18,560	7,609	4,916
People per Square Mile	32.6	134.9	108.2	73.7
High School Graduates	87.8%	85.2%	87.5%	87.9%
College/Adv. Degree	27.1 %	20.7%	26.2%	26.6%
Median Household Income	$35,811	$36,498	$35,774	$38,686
Aver. Temp. Range, °F	Ellsworth	Augusta	Rockland	Wiscasset★★
January	30.1 to 10.5	27.6 to 10.4	32 to 10.2	30.1 to 10.4
April	51.7 to 32.3	52.1 to 34.4	50.3 to 33.6	52.4 to 34.2
July	77.9 to 57	79 to 60.1	79.9 to 57.1	77.9 to 59.3
October	57.8 to 39.3	575 to 39.8	56.2 to 39.6	58.4 to 39.4
Crime Rate per Thousand (2000)	23.78	23.72	19.07	15.41

★Most recent census estimate.

★★Based on the average temperatures at Brunswick, the nearest National Weather Service station.

County	Oxford	Penobscot	Piscataquis	Sagadahoc
Population 2004★	56,614	148,196	17,525	36,927
Population 1990	52,606	146,601	18,653	33,535
Population 1980	49,043	137,015	17,634	28,795
Largest Town (2000 pop.)	Rumford	Bangor	Dover-Foxcroft	Bath
	6,472	31,473	4,211	9,266
People per Square Mile	26.3	42.7	4.3	138.6
High School Graduates	82.4%	85.7%	80.3%	88%
College/Adv. Degree	15.7%	20.3%	13.3%	25%
Median Household Income	$33,435	$34,274	$28,250	$41,908
Aver. Temp. Range, °F	Rumford	Bangor	Dover-Foxcroft	Bath★★
January	27.2 to 5.8	26.7 to 8.2	24.2 to 2.4	30.1 to 10.4
April	52.3 to 31.2	50.9 to 32.8	49.5 to 28.8	52.4 to 34.2
July	79.6 to 56.4	78.1 to 58.3	78.6 to 54.5	77.9 to 59.3
October	57.5 to 36.6	56.9 to 38.7	55.6 to 33.6	58.4 to 39.4
Crime Rate per Thousand (2000)	21.89	29.02	26.15	23.9

★Most recent census estimate.

County	Somerset	Waldo	Washington	York
Population 2004★	51,584	38,392	33,558	200,359
Population 1990	49,767	33,018	35,308	164,587
Population 1980	45,049	28,414	34,963	139,739
Largest Town	Skowhegan	Belfast	Calais	Sanford
(2000 pop.)	8,824	6,381	3,447	20,942
People per Square Mile	13	49.7	13.2	188.4
High School Graduates	80.8%	84.6%	79.9%	86.5%
College/Adv. Degree	11.8%	22.3%	14.7%	22.9%
Median Household Income	$30,731	$33,986	$25,869	$43,630
Aver. Temp. Range, °F	Madison	Belfast	Eastport	Sanford
January	26.8 to 2.1	32 to 10.7	29.7 to 13.9	32.5 to 10.4
April	51.2 to 30.1	53.9 to 32.3	48.5 to 32.8	57.3 to 32
July	79.1 to 55.6	79.9 to 57.1	72.9 to 53	83.2 to 57.1
October	57.2 to 34.7	59.9 to 38.9	55.7 to 40.8	62.5 to 37.1
Crime Rate per Thousand (2000)	28.74	8.48	22.57	25.67

★Most recent census estimate.

APPENDIX 2

Quality Medical Care—Maine Hospitals

Data provided by *Down East* magazine.
Note: Numbers in parentheses following hospital names indicate number of acute care beds in that facility.

Augusta

Maine General Medical Center
(287)
6 East Chestnut St.
Augusta, ME 04330
207-626-1000

Bangor

Acadia Hospital *(100)*
268 Stillwater Ave.
Bangor, ME 04402-0422
207-973-6100

Eastern Maine Medical Center
(411)
189 State St., P.O. Box 101
Bangor, ME 04402-0404
207-973-7000

St. Joseph Hospital *(82)*
360 Broadway
Bangor, ME 01401
207-262-1000

Bar Harbor

Mount Desert Island Hospital *(25)*
10 Wayman Lane, P.O. Box 8
Bar Harbor, ME 01609-0008
207-288-5081

Belfast

Waldo County General Hospital
(25)
118 Northport Ave., P.O. Box
287
Belfast, ME 04915
207-338-2500

Blue Hill

Blue Hill Memorial Hospital *(25)*
Water St.
Blue Hill, ME 04614
207-374-2836

Biddeford

Southern Maine Medical Center
(150)
1 Medical Center Drive, P.O. Box
626
Biddeford, ME 04005
207-283-7000

Boothbay Harbor

St. Andrews Hospital *(20)*
6 St. Andrews Dr., P.O. Box 417
Boothbay Harbor, ME 04538
207-633-2121

Bridgton

Northern Cumberland Memorial
Hospital *(25)*
10 Hospital Dr. (off South High
St.), P.O. Box 230
Bridgton, ME 04009
207-647-6000

Brunswick

Mid Coast Hospital *(73)*
123 Medical Center Dr.
Brunswick. ME 04011
207-729-0181

Parkview Hospital *(55)*
329 Maine St.
Brunswick, ME 04011
207-373-2000

Calais

Calais Regional Hospital *(25)*
22 Hospital Lane
Calais, ME 04619
207-454-7521

Caribou

Cary Medical Center *(23)*
163 Van Buren Rd.
Caribou, ME 04736
207-498-3111

Damariscotta

Miles Memorial Hospital *(35)*
35 Miles St.
Damariscotta, ME 04543
207-563-1234

Dover-Foxcroft

Mayo Regional Hospital *(25)*
897 West Main St.
Dover-Foxcroft, ME 04426
207-564-4342

Ellsworth

Maine Coast Memorial Hospital
(64)
50 Union St.
Ellsworth, ME 04605
207-667-5311

Farmington

Franklin Memorial Hospital *(70)*
1 Hospital Dr.
Farmington. ME 04938
207-778-6031

Fort Kent

Northern Maine Medical Center
  (48)
191 East Main St.
Fort Kent, ME 04743
207-834-3155

Greenville

C.A. Dean Memorial Hospital *(14)*
Pritham Ave., P.O. Box 1129
Greenville. ME 04441
207-695-5200

Houlton

Houlton Regional Hospital *(25)*
20 Hartford St.
Houlton, ME 04730
207-532-2900

Lewiston

Central Maine Medical Center
  (250)
300 Main St.
Lewiston, ME 04240
207-795-0111

St. Mary's Regional Medical Center *(233)*
P.O. Box 291
Lewiston, ME 04243-0291
207-777-8100

Lincoln

Penobscot Valley Hospital *(25)*
7 Transalpine Rd., Box 368
Lincoln, ME 04457-0368
207-794-3321

Machias

Down East Community Hospital
  (25)
RR 1, Box 11
Machias, ME 04654
207-255-3356

Millinocket

Millinocket Regional Hospital *(15)*
200 Somerset St.
Millinocket, ME 04462
207-723-5161

Norway

Stephens Memorial Hospital *(50)*
181 Main St.
Norway, ME 04268
207-743-5933

Pittsfield

Sebasticook Valley Hospital *(25)*
99 Grove Hill
Pittsfield, ME 04967
207-487-5141

Portland

New England Rehabilitation Hospital *(100)*
335 Brighton Avenue, Unit 201
Portland, ME 04102
207-775-4000

Maine Medical Center *(605)*
22 Bramhall St.
Portland, ME 04102
207-871-0111

Mercy Hospital *(200)*
144 State St.
Portland, ME 04101
207-879-3000

Presque Isle

Aroostook Medical Center *(72)*
140 Academy St., Box 151
Presque Isle, ME 04769
207-768-4000

Rockport

Penobscot Bay Medical Center
(109)
6 Glen Cove Dr.
Rockport, ME 04856-4240
207-596-8000

Rumford

Rumford Community Hospital
(25)
120 Franklin St.
Rumford, ME 04276
207-364-4581

Sanford

Goodall Hospital *(55)*
25 June St.
Sanford, ME 04073
207-321-4310

Skowhegan

Redington-Fairview General Hospital *(65)*
46 Fairview Ave., P.O. Box 468
Skowhegan, ME 04976
207-474-5121

South Portland

Spring Harbor Hospital *(100)*
175 Running Hill Rd.
S. Portland, ME 04106
207-761-2200

Waterville

Inland Hospital *(45)*
200 Kennedy Memorial Dr.
Waterville, ME 04901
207-861-3000

Maine General Medical Center
(Seton and Thayer units) *(350)*
149 North Main St.
Waterville, ME 04901
207-872-1000

Westbrook

Mercy Westbrook *(30)*
40 Park Rd.
Westbrook, ME 01092
207-854-8000

York

York Hospital *(72)*
15 Hospital Dr.
York, ME 03909
207-363-4321

APPENDIX 3

Local Issues—Maine Newspapers

Data provided by *Down East* magazine.

DAILIES

Augusta

Kennebec Journal
274 Western Avenue
Augusta, ME 04332
207-623-3811
www.kjonline.com

Bangor

Bangor Daily News
P.O. Box 1329
Bangor, ME 04402
207-990-8000
www.bangornews.com

Biddeford

Journal Tribune
P.O. Box 627
Biddeford, ME 04005
207-282-1535
www.journaltribune.com

Brunswick

The Times Record
P.O. Box 10
Brunswick, ME 04011
207-729-3311
www.timcsrecord.com

Lewiston

The Sun-Journal
P.O. Box 4100
Lewiston, ME 04243
207-784-5411
www.sunjoumal.corn

Waterville

Central Maine Morning Sentinel
31 Front Street
Waterville, ME 04901
207-873-3341
www.onlinesentinel.com

Portland

Portland Press Herald
390 Congress St.
Portland, ME 04104
207-791-6650
www.prcssherald.com

WEEKLIES AND OTHERS

Augusta

Capital Weekly
P.O. Box 2788
Augusta, ME 04338
207-621-6000
www.courierpub.com

Bar Harbor

The Bar Harbor Times
P.O. Box 68
Bar Harbor, ME 04609
207-288-3311
www.courierpub.corn

Bath

Coastal Journal
P.O. Box 705
Bath, ME 04530
207-443-6241
www.coastaljournal.com

Belfast

Republican Journal
P.O. Box 327, 71 High St.
Belfast, ME 04915
207-338-3333
www.courierpub.com

The Waldo Independent
P.O. Box 228
Belfast, ME 04915
207-338-5100
www.courierpub.com

Village Soup Citizen
48-4 Marshall Wharf
Belfast, ME 04915
207-338-0484
waldo.villagesoup.com

Bethel

The Bethel Citizen
P.O. Box 109
Bethel, ME 04217
207-824-2444
www.bethelcitizen.com

Biddeford

*Biddeford-Saco-Old Orchard Beach
   Courier*
P.O. Box 1894
Biddeford, ME 04005
207-282-4337

Blue Hill

The Weekly Packet
P.O. Box 646
Blue Hill, ME 01611
207-374-2341
www.weeklypacket.com

Boothbay Harbor

The Boothbay Register
P.O. Box 357
Boothbay Harbor, ME 04538
207-633-4620
www.boothbayregister.maine.com

Bridgton

The Bridgton News
P.O. Box 244
Bridgton, ME 04009
207-647-2851

Bucksport

The Enterprise
P.O. Box 829
Bucksport, ME 04416
207-469-6722

Calais

The Calais Advertiser
P.O. Box 660
Calais, ME 04619
207-454-3561
www.the-calais-advertiser.com

Downeast Times
332 North Street
Calais, ME 04619
207-454-2884
www.downeastwebs.com

Camden

The Camden Herald
56 Elm Street
Camden, ME 04813
207-236-8511
www.courierpub.com

Village Soup Times
21 Elm Street
Camden, ME 04843
207-236-8468
camden.village soup.com

Cape Elizabeth

The Cape Courier
P.O. Box 6242
Cape Elizabeth, ME 04107
207-767-5023
www.capecourier.com

Caribou

Aroostook Republican & News
P.O. Box 608
Caribou, ME 04736
207-496-3251

Castine

Castine Patriot
P.O. Box 205
Castine, ME 04421
207-326-9300
www.castinepatriot.com

Cutler

The Downeast Coastal Press
2413 Culler Rd.
Cutler. ME 04626
207-259-7751

Damariscotta

Lincoln County News
P.O. Box 36
Damariscotta, ME 04543
207-563-3171
www.mainelincolncountynews.
   com

Lincoln County Weekly
P.O. Box 1287
Damariscotta, ME 04543
207-563-5006
www.couricrpub.com

Dexter

The Eastern Gazette
P.O. Box 306
Dexter, ME 04930
207-924-7402

Dover-Foxcroft

Piscataquis Observer
P.O. Box 30
Dover-Foxcroft, ME 04426
207-564-8355

Eastport

The Quoddy Tides (twice monthly)
P.O. Box 213
Eastport, ME 04631
207-853-4806
www.quoddytides.com

Ellsworth

The Ellsworth American
P.O. Box 509
Ellsworth, ME 04605
207-667-2576
www.wellsworthamerican.com

Falmouth

Falmouth Forecaster
317 Foreside Rd.
Falmouth, ME 04105
207-781-3661
www.theforecaster.net

Farmington

Franklin Journal (twice weekly)
P.O. Box 750
Farmington, ME 04938
207-778-2075

Gorham

Gorham Times
P.O. Box 401
Gorham, ME 04038
207-839-8390
www.gorhamtimes.com

Gray

The Gray News
P.O. Box 433
Gray, ME 01039
207-657-2200
www.graynews.maine.com

Greenville

Moosehead Messenger
P.O. Box 100
Greenville, ME 04441
207-695-3077
www.moosemessenger.corn

Houlton

Houlton Pioneer Times
P.O. Box 456
Houlton, ME 04730
207-532-2281

Islesboro

Islesboro Island News (six per year)
P.O. Box 104
Islesboro, ME 04848
207-734-6921
www.islesboronews.com

Kennebunk

York County Coast Star
P.O. Box 979
Kennebunk, ME 04043
207-985·2961
www.seacoastonline.com/news/
yorkstar

Kingfield

The Irregular
P.O. Box 616
Kingfield, ME 04947
207-265-2773
www.news.mywebpal.com/indcx.
cfm?pnpid=282

Lincoln

Lincoln News
P.O. Box 35
Lincoln, ME 04457
207-794-6532
www.mainlincolncountynews.com

Livermore Falls

Livermore Falls Advertiser
P.O. Box B
Livermore Falls, ME 04254
207-897-4321

Lubec

The Lubec Light
R.R. 2, Box 380
Lubec, ME 04652
207-733-2939

Machias

The County Wide
P.O. Box 497
Machias, ME 04654
207-564-7518

Machias Valley News Observer
P.O. Box 357
Machias, ME 04654
207-255-6561

Madawaska

Saint John Valley Times
P.O. Box 419
Madawaska, ME 04756
207-728-3336

Millinocket

Katahdin Times
202 Penobscot Ave., P.O. Box 330
Millinocket, ME 01162
207-723-8118

New Gloucester

New Gloucester News
PO. Box 102
New Gloucester, ME 04260
207-926-4036
www.newgloucesternews.com

Norway

Advertiser Democrat
P.O. Box 269
Norway, ME 04268
207-743-7011
www.advertiserdemocrat.com

The Bear Facts (twice monthly)
P.O. Rox 718
Norway, ME 04268
207-583-2851

Old Town

Penobscot Times
P.O. Box 568
Old Town, ME 04468
207-827-4451

Portland

Maine Sunday Telegram
390 Congress Street
Portland, ME 04101
207-775-6601
www.portland.com

Presque Isle

The Star-Herald
P.O. Box. 110
Presque Isle, ME 04769
207-768-5431

Rangeley

Rangeley Highlander
P.O. Box 542
Rangeley, ME 04970
207-864-3756

Rockland

The Courier Gazette (three per week)
P.O. Box 249
Rockland, ME 04841
207-594-4401
www.courierpub.com

The Free Press
8 North Main Street, Suite 101
Rockland, ME 04841
207-596-0055
www.freepressonline.com

Rumford

Rumford Falls Times
P.O. Box 490
Rumford, ME 04276
207-364-7893
www.rumfordfallstimes.com

APPENDIX 4

Chambers of Commerce

Data provided by the Maine Office of Tourism.

Augusta

Kennebec Valley Chamber of Commerce
P.O. Box 676, Augusta 04332-0676
207-623-4559

Bangor Region Chamber of Commerce
519 Main Street, Bangor 04402-1143
207-947-0307

Bar Harbor Chamber of Commerce
P.O. Box 158, Bar Harbor 04609
207-288-5103

Bath

Chamber of Commerce of the Bath-Brunswick Region
45 Front Street, Bath 04530
207-443-9751

Belfast Area Chamber of Commerce
P.O. Box 58, Belfast 04915
207-338-5900

Bethel Area Chamber of Commerce
P.O. Box 1247, Bethel 04217
207-824-2282

Biddeford-Saco Chamber of Commerce
110 Main Street, Suite 1202, Saco 04072
207-282-1567

Bingham

Upper Kennebec Valley Chamber of Commerce
P.O. Box 491, Bingham 04920
207-672-4100

Boothbay Region Information Center
P.O. Box 187, Boothbay 04537
207-633-4743

Boothbay Harbor Region Chamber of Commerce
P.O. Box 356, Boothbay Harbor 04538
207-633-2353

Bridgton

Greater Bridgton Lakes Region Chamber of Commerce
P.O. Box 236, Bridgton 04009
207-647-3472

Brunswick

Chamber of Commerce of the Bath-Brunswick Region
59 Pleasant Street, Brunswick 04011
207-725-8797

Bucksport Bay Area Chamber of Commerce
P.O. Box 1880, Bucksport 04416
207-469-6818

Calais Regional Chamber of Commerce
P.O. Box 368, Calais 04619
207-454-2308

Camden-Rockport-Lincolnville Chamber of Commerce
P.O. Box 919, Camden 01843
207-236-4404

Caribou Chamber of Commerce
111 High Street, Caribou 04736
207-498-6156

Sugarloaf Area Information Center
RR 1, Box 2151, Carrabassett Valley 04947
207-235-2100

Damariscotta Region Chamber of Commerce
P.O. Box 13, Damariscotta 04543
207-563-8340

Damariscotta Region Information Bureau
P.O. Box 217, Damariscotta 04543
207-563-3175

Dover-Foxcroft

Southern Piscataquis County Chamber of Commerce
P.O. Box 376, Dover-Foxcroft 04426
207-561-7533

Eastport Area Chamber of Commerce
P.O. Box 254, Eastport 04631
207-853-4644

Ellsworth Area Chamber of Commerce
P.O. Box 267, Ellsworth 01605
207-667-2617

Farmington

Greater Farmington Chamber of Commerce
RR 4, Box 5091, Farmington 04938
207-778-4215

Fort Fairfield Chamber of Commerce
128 Main Street, Suite 4, Fort Fairfield 04742
207-472-3802

Fort Kent

Greater Fort Kent Area Chamber of Commerce
P.O. Box 430, Fort Kent 04743
207-834-5354

Freeport Merchants Association
P.O. Box 452, Freeport 04032
207-865-1212

Greenville

Moosehead Lake Region Chamber of Commerce
P.O. Box 581, Greenville 04441
207-695-2702

Houlton Chamber of Commerce
109 Main Street, Houlton 04730
207-532-4216

Island Falls

Northern Katahdin Valley Regional Chamber of Commerce
P.O. Box 374, Island Falls 04717
207-463-2077

Jackman-Moose River Region Chamber of Commerce
P.O. Box 368, Jackman 04945
207-668-4171

Kennebunk-Kennebunkport Chamber of Commerce
P.O. Box 740, Kennebunk 04043
207-967-0857

Kittery

Gateway to Maine
P.O. Box 526, Kittery 03904
207-439-7545

Lewiston

Androscoggin County Chamber of Commerce
P.O. Box 59, Lewiston 04243-0059
207-783-2249

Limestone Chamber of Commerce
291 Main Street, Limestone 04750
207-325-4025

Lincoln Chamber of Commerce
P.O. Box 164, Lincoln 04457
207-794-8065

Machias Bay Area Chamber of Commerce
P.O. Box 606, Machias 04564
207-255-4402

Madawaska

Greater Madawaska Chamber of Commerce
378 Main Street, Madawaska 04756
207-728-7000

Maine Chamber and Business Alliance
7 University Drive, Augusta 04330-9412
207-623-4568

Millinocket

Katahdin Area Chamber of Commerce
1029 Central Street, Millinocket 04462
207-723-4443

Naples Information Center
P.O. Box 112, Naples 04055
207-693-3285

Mount Desert Chamber of Commerce
P.O. Box 675, Northeast Harbor 01662
207-276-5040

Ogunquit Chamber of Commerce
P.O. Box 2289, Ogunquit 03907
207-646-2939

Old Orchard Beach Chamber of Commerce
P.O. Box 600, Old Orchard Beach 04064
207-934-2500

Portland

Convention and Visitors Bureau of Greater Portland
305 Commercial Street, Portland 04101
207-772-5800

Presque Isle Area Chamber of Commerce
P.O. Box 672, Presque Isle 04769
207-761-6561

Rangeley Lakes Region Chamber of Commerce
P.O. Box 317, Rangeley 04970
207-864-5571

Rockland-Thomaston Area Chamber of Commerce
P.O. Box 508, Rockland 04841
207-596-0376

Rumford

River Valley Chamber of Commerce
P.O. Box 598. Rumford 04276
207-364-3241

St. Francis Chamber of Commerce
P.O. Box 123, St Francis 04774
207-398-3431

Sanford Springvale Chamber of Commerce and Economic Development
261 Main Street, Sanford 04073
207-324-4280

Skowhegan Area Chamber of Commerce
P.O. Box 326, Skowhegan 04976
207-474-3621

Oxford Hills Chamber of Commerce
P.O. Box 167, South Paris 04281
207-713-2281

Southwest Harbor–Tremont
Chamber of Commerce
P.O. Box 1143, Southwest Harbor
04679
207–244–9261

Deer Isle–Stonington Chamber of
Commerce
P.O. Box 459, Stonington 04681
207–348–6124

Unity

Waldo County Regional Chamber
of Commerce
P.O. Box 577, Unity 04974
207–948–5050

Van Buren

Greater Van Buren Chamber of
Commerce
65 Main Street, Van Buren 04785
207–868–5059

Waldoboro Town Office
P.O. Box J, Waldoboro 04572
207–832–5369

Waterville

Mid-Maine Chamber of Com-
merce
P.O. Box 142, Waterville 04903–
0142
207–873–3315

Wells Chamber of Commerce
P.O. Box 356, Wells 04090
207–646–2451

Wilton Chamber of Commerce
P.O. Box 934, Wilton 04294
207–645–3932

Windham Chamber of
Commerce
P.O. Box 1015, Windham 04062
207–892–8265

Yarmouth Chamber of Commerce
158 Main Street, Yarmouth 04096
207–846–3984

Yorks Chamber of Commerce
571 US Route 1, York 03909
207–363–4422

APPENDIX 5

Retirement Communities

Every year more retirement communities are being built or expanded. Please call or write the individual facilities for their latest information. (Data as of March 2000, provided by *Town East* magazine.)

The communities listed here all provide housekeeping services and at least one meal per day, and most can provide transportation.

Key to abbreviations in the Types of Units column:
IA = independent apartments
C = cottages
A = Alzheimer's units
LT = long-term-care beds
AL = assisted-living units

Facility	Number of Residents	Distance to Hospital (in miles)	Rent, Purchase, or Both	Types of Units
Auburn				
Clover Health Care 440 Minot Ave. Auburn, ME 04210 207-784-3573 www.mainecare.com	270	3	R	IA, AL, LT, A

189

Facility	Number of Residents	Distance to Hospital (in miles)	Rent, Purchase, or Both	Types of Units
Schooner Retirement Community 200 Stetson Rd. Auburn, ME 04210 207-784-2900; 800-924-9997 www.schoonerestates.com	180	3	R	IA, AL, LT

Bangor

Park East Retirement Villa 146 Balsam Dr. Bangor, ME 04401 207-947-7992 www.parkeastapts.com	22	1	R	IA
Boyd Place 21 Boyd St. Bangor, ME 04401 207-941-2837	85	0.5	R	IA, AL
Sunbury Village 922 Ohio St. Bangor, ME 04401 207-262-9600 www.sunburyvillage.net	138	2	R	IA

Bar Harbor

Birch Bay Village 25 Village Inn Rd. Bar Harbor, ME 04609 207-288-8014 www.birchbayinfo.com	130	4	B	IA, C, AL, A

Facility	Number of Residents	Distance to Hospital (in miles)	Rent, Purchase, or Both	Types of Units
Belfast				
Harbor Hill 2 Footbridge Rd. Belfast, ME 04915 207-338-5307 www.sandyriverhealth.com	85	3	R	AL, LT, A
Penobscot Shores 10 Shoreland Dr. Belfast, ME 04915 207-338-2332 www.penobscotshores.com	74	0.25	B	IA, C
Blue Hill				
Parker Ridge Retirement Community 63 Parker Ridge Ln Blue Hill, ME 04614 207-374-2306 www.parkerridge.com	71	3	B	IA, C, AL
Boothbay Harbor				
St. Andrews Village 145 Emery Lane Boothbay Harbor, ME 04538 207-633-0920 www.standrewsvillage.com	150	1.5	B	IA, C, AL, LT, A

Facility	Number of Residents	Distance to Hospital (in miles)	Rent, Purchase, or Both	Types of Units
Brewer				
Ellen M. Leach Memorial Home P.O. Box 359 Brewer, ME 04412 207-989-7890 www.leachmemorialhome.org	66	1.5	R	IA
Brunswick				
Sunnybrook Village 25 Thornton Way Brunswick, ME 04011 207-729-8033; 800-729-8033 www.sunnybrookvillage.com	51	1	R	IA, AL, LT
Thornton Oaks 25 Thornton Way Brunswick, ME 04011 207-729-8033; 800-729-8033 www.thorntonoaks.com	175	4.8	P	IA, C, AL, LT, A
Camden				
Camden Gardens 110 Mechanic St. Camden, ME 04843 207-236-0154	12	5	B	IA, C
Quarry Hill 30 Community Dr. Camden, ME 04843 207-230-6116 www.quarryhill.org	225	6	B	IA, C, AL, LT, A

Facility	Number of Residents	Distance to Hospital (in miles)	Rent, Purchase, or Both	Types of Units
Cape Elizabeth				
Village Crossings at Cape Elizabeth 78 Scott Dyer Rd. Cape Elizabeth, ME 04107 207-799-7332; 888-860-6914 www.carematrix.com	54	4	R	AL
Damariscotta				
Chase Point Assisted Living 65 Schooner St. Damariscotta, ME 04543 207-563-5523 www.mileshealthcare.org/ schooner	42	0	R	AL
Schooner Cove 65 Schooner St. Damariscotta, ME 04543 207-563-5523 www.mileshealthcare.org/ schooner	59	0.1	B	IA
Falmouth				
OceanView at Falmouth 20 Blueberry Lane Falmouth, ME 04105 207-781-4460 www.oceanviewrc.com	250	6	P	IA, C, IL

Facility	Number of Residents	Distance to Hospital (in miles)	Rent, Purchase, or Both	Types of Units
Farmington				
Orchard Park Rehabilitation and Living Ctr. 12 North St. Farmington, ME 04938 207-778-4416; 800-260-4416	13	5	R	IA, AL
Gorham				
Gorham House 50 New Portland Rd. Gorham, ME 04038 207-839-5757 www.mainecare.com	165	12	R	IA, AL, LT, A
Hallowell				
Granite Hill Estates 60 Balsam Dr. Hallowell, ME 04347 207-626-7786; 888-321-1119 www.granitehillestates.com	150	2	P	IA, C
Hampden				
Avalon Village 50 Foxglove Dr. Hampden, ME 04444 207-862-5100; 800-950-0037 www.avalon-maine.com	94	4	B	IA, C

Facility	Number of Residents	Distance to Hospital (in miles)	Rent, Purchase, or Both	Types of Units
Houlton				
Madigan Estates 93 Military St. Houlton, ME 04730 207-532-6593 www.madiganestates.com	134	1.5	R	IA, AL, LT, A
Kennebunk				
Atria Kennebunk 1 Penny Lane Kennebunk, ME 04043 207-985-5866 www.atriacom.com	82	1.5	R	AL, A
Huntington Common 1 Huntington Common Dr. Kennebunk, ME 04043 207-985-2810; 800-585-0533 www.huntingtoncommon. com	200	7	R	IA, C, AL, C
The Farragut at Kennebunk 106 Farragut Way Kennebunk, ME 04043 207-985-9740 www.thefarragut.com	70	4.5	B	IA, C
Lewiston				
Montello Heights 550 College St. Lewiston, ME 04240 207-786-7149	80	2	R	IA

Facility	Number of Residents	Distance to Hospital (in miles)	Rent, Purchase, or Both	Types of Units
Newcastle				
Lincoln Home 22 River Rd. Newcastle, ME 04553 207-563-3350	40	1	R	IA, AL
Orono				
Dirigo Pines Retirement Community 9 Alumni Dr. Orono, ME 04473 866-344-3400 www.dirigopines.com	98	0.1	R	IA, C, AL, LT, A
Portland				
The Atrium at Cedars 640 Ocean Ave. Portland, ME 04103 207-775-4111 www.thecedarsportland.org	60	2.5	P	IA, AL
The Park Danforth 777 Stevens Ave. Portland, ME 04103 207-797-7710 www.parkdanforth.com	170	4	R	IA, AL
Seventy-Five State Street 75 State St. Portland, ME 04101 207-772-2675 www.75state.org	170	0.1	R	IA, AL

Facility	Number of Residents	Distance to Hospital (in miles)	Rent, Purchase, or Both	Types of Units
The Woods at Canco 257 Canco Rd. Portland, ME 04103 207-772-4777	148	5	R	IA, C

Presque Island

Leisure Garden Apartments 4 Dewberry Dr. Presque Isle, ME 04769 207-764-7322 www.ainop.com/lgardens/	140	0.1	R	IA, AL

Rockland

Bartlett Woods 20 Bartlett Dr. Rockland, ME 04841 207-594-2745 www.bartlettwoods.com	57	2.5	B	IA, C

Saco

Atlantic Heights Retirement Community One Harbor Dr. Saco, ME 04072 207-283-3022; 800-874-6990 www.atlanticheightsretirement.com	231	4	R	C, LT, A
The Monarch Center 392 Main St. Saco, ME 04072 207-284-0900 www.themonarchcenter.com	40	5	R	AL, A

Facility	Number of Residents	Distance to Hospital (in miles)	Rent, Purchase, or Both	Types of Units
Wardwell Retirement Neighborhood 43 Middle St. Saco, ME 04072 207-284-7061	98	2.5	R	IA, AL

Scarborough

Piper Shores 15 Piper Rd. Scarborough, ME 04074 207-883-8700; 888-333-8711 www.pipershores.org	350	7	Life Care	IA, C, AL, LT

Topsham

The Highlands 26 Elm St. Topsham, ME 04086 207-725-2650; 888-760-1042 www.highlandsrc.com	300	5	B	IA, C, AL, A

Waterville

Woodlands Assisted Living of Waterville 141 West River Rd. Waterville, ME 04901 207-861-5685 www.woodlandsofwaterville.com	129	1	R	IA, AL, A

Facility	Number of Residents	Distance to Hospital (in miles)	Rent, Purchase, or Both	Types of Units
Yarmouth				
Bay Square at Yarmouth 27 Forest Falls Dr. Yarmouth, ME 04096 207-846-0044; 888-374-6700 www.benchmarkquality.com	60	12	R	AL, A
York				
Sentry Hill 2 Victoria Ct. York, ME 03909 207-363-5116 www.sentryhill.com	160	0.5	B	IA, C, AL, A